The Heinle & Heinle TOEFL® Test Assistant:
Vocabulary

Milada Broukal
Glendale Community College

Heinle & Heinle Publishers
An International Thomson Publishing Company
Boston, MA 02116 U.S.A.

TOEFL® and TWE® are registered trademarks of Educational Testing Service. There is no connection between Heinle & Heinle Publishers and Educational Testing Service.

The publication of *The Heinle & Heinle TOEFL® Test Assistant: Vocabulary* was directed by the members of the Global Innovations Publishing Team at Heinle & Heinle:

David C. Lee, Editorial Director
Martha Liebs, Production Editor
John F. McHugh, Market Development Director

Also participating in the publication of this program were:

Publisher: Stanley J. Galek
Editorial Production Manager: Elizabeth Holthaus
Project Manager: Publication Services
Assistant Editor: Kenneth Mattsson
Associate Marketing Manager: Donna Hamilton
Production Assistant: Maryellen Eschmann
Manufacturing Coordinator: Mary Beth Hennebury
Interior Designer: Publication Services
Cover Illustrator: George Abe
Cover Designer: Kimberly Wedlake

Manufactured in the United States of America

Library of Congress Cataloging in Publication Data
Broukal, Milada.
    The Heinle & Heinle TOEFL test assistant : vocabulary / Milada
Broukal.
       p.   cm.
    Includes index.
    ISBN 0-8384-4280-3
    1. Test of English as a foreign language—Study guides.
2. English language—Textbooks for foreign speakers.   3. Vocabulary—
Examinations—Study guides.   I. Title.   II. Title: Heinle and
Heinle TOEFL Test Assistant.
PE1122.B694   1994
428′.0076—dc20   94-12306
                                                                CIP

ISBN: 0-8384-4280-3
10 9

Contents

To the Teacher

The Heinle & Heinle TOEFL® Test Assistant: Vocabulary is a vocabulary building text that prepares students to meet the vocabulary needs in all sections of the TOEFL® test; i.e., Listening Comprehension, Structure and Written Expression, and Vocabulary and Reading Comprehension, in a variety of ways.

Each section of the TOEFL® test has different vocabulary needs. The Listening Comprehension section requires vocabulary in the form of idioms, phrasal verbs, and everyday and specific vocabulary. The Structure and Written Expression section tests knowledge of suffixes, and of confusing words. The Vocabulary and Reading Comprehension section requires looking for contextual clues that reveal the meaning of a word. When contextual clues are not helpful, a knowledge of synonyms, roots, and prefixes will help to find the meaning. It is, therefore, important to address all these needs in a comprehensive TOEFL® test vocabulary book.

Each chapter of *The Heinle & Heinle TOEFL® Test Assistant: Vocabulary* addresses the different vocabulary needs for the test. The vocabulary is contextualized in the beginning of each chapter in a reading passage or conversation. These do not replicate the passages or conversations found on the test because their purpose is to promote classroom activity and learning skills. Similarly, in Chapter 1, "Words in Context," vocabulary is contextualized in passages of lower overall difficulty than those found on the actual exam, since its aim is to strengthen the vocabulary teaching aspect of the book. The readings are, however, selected from areas of readings covered by the TOEFL® test such as biology, physical science, history, art, and social science.

 ## Structure of Each Chapter

- **Presentation**
  A reading or listening passage, a dialogue, or a structure passage presents the vocabulary to be studied in the unit in contextualized form.

- **Comprehension questions**
  Comprehension questions follow the passages or dialogues. These questions are followed by tasks to encourage students to use contextual clues and relate words with one another. Students can work alone, in groups, or in pairs.

- **Strategies for vocabulary development**
  Strategies are presented that deal with the particular vocabulary building focus of the chapter.

- **Exercises**

  There are a variety of exercise types ranging from multiple choice, blank filling, correcting errors, completing word lists, using the dictionary to find out meanings, and so on. These exercises can be done in the classroom with students interacting in pairs or groups or they can be assigned as homework.

- **End of chapter tests**

  The end of unit test focuses on the vocabulary taught in the unit. The question types are similar to those found on the TOEFL® test.

 # How to Use This Book

1. **Order of presentation**

   The units in this book do not have to be covered in the order presented. You can either follow the order of the book or choose the units that tie in with your curriculum.

2. **Classroom use**

   The introductory passages and/or dialogues with the questions and tasks that follow can be used for interactive work, with students working in groups or pairs to answer the questions. If more listening skills need to be worked on, you can read the reading passages and the dialogues aloud. After going over the strategies with the students, the exercises that follow can be either worked on in the classroom, or if there is not enough time to cover them in class you can assign them as homework.

3. **Use of dictionaries**

   The use of a good dictionary is encouraged, however it is recommended that the dictionary act as a reinforcement after the student has tried to work out the meaning of a word by himself/herself through context or other clues.

To the Student

This book will help you to build your vocabulary for all sections of the TOEFL®. Study the chapters in this book, but don't stop there. Vocabulary learning is a lifelong process; make sure you learn some new words every day. The following are some strategies for building your vocabulary whether you are working alone or in the classroom.

 ## Strategies for Vocabulary Building

- **Read as much as you can**
  By reading as many magazines, fiction and non-fiction books, and journals as you can, you will encounter new words. You can guess the meanings of many of these words by their context—that is, you will get a clue to the meaning from the words that surround the new word. If you are still not sure, you can look up the word in a dictionary to check if you were right.

- **Use a dictionary**
  Buy a good dictionary, preferably a college-level dictionary. The dictionary should be all English, not a bilingual one. A good dictionary should include the following information about a word:

    its pronunciation

    its part of speech (noun, adjective, verb)

    a clear, simple definition

    an example of the word used in a sentence or phrase

    its origin (root, prefix)

  You can also use a pocket dictionary if you travel back and forth to classes.

- **Learn roots, prefixes, and suffixes**
  Roots and prefixes from Latin and Greek make up many English words. It has been estimated that more than half of all English words come from Latin and Greek. Prefixes are added to the beginning of a root and suffixes are added to the end to modify the meaning of words. Learning these will help you increase your vocabulary.

- **Learn from listening**
  Listening to good programs on the radio and television as well as to people who speak English well is another way of improving your vocabulary. Since you cannot always ask the speaker to tell you what a particular word means, write down the words and look them up later.

- **Use a dictionary of synonyms and antonyms**
  Synonyms are words that have almost the same meaning; antonyms are words that have almost the opposite meaning. Knowing the synonyms and antonyms of a word will expand your vocabulary. Some dictionaries of synonyms and antonyms explain each synonym and how it differs in meaning from other synonyms. Since no two words have the exact same meaning, this is very useful for you.

- **Make your own word list**
  Get a notebook for your vocabulary study and use it to create your own word list. Whenever you read and come across a word you don't know, write it down in your notebook together with the sentence in which you found it. Try to work out the meaning of the word from its context. Then look the word up in a dictionary and write the definition in your notebook. Also, write down any other information such as the root of the word, and see how it is connected to the meaning. Lastly, write your own sentence using the word. Writing will help you remember the word and its meaning. Try to add a new word to your list every day.

- **Create your own theme groups**
  Words are easier to remember and learn when you group words with similar meanings under a theme. For example,

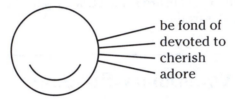

be fond of
devoted to
cherish
adore

Then you can make another theme with the opposite.

detest
loathe
abhor
repel
despise
disgust

- **Use your new words**
  Using your new words whether it be in speaking or writing is an important step in learning them.

Text Credits

I would like to acknowledge the sources for some of the passages used in this text. In some cases several sources were used for a passage, in others the passage was slightly changed in content or style. The following is a list of the sources used:

Chapter 1

The passages in the first ten readings are based on information in Young Students *Learning Library,* Weekly Reader Books, Middletown, Connecticut. The passage on Grandma Moses and the passage on Pop Art is based on information in *The Story of American Painting* by Abraham A. Davidson, Harry N. Abrams, Inc., Publishers, New York, 1974. The passage on the bristlecone pines is based on information in *Arid Lands* by Jake Page, Time-Life Books, Alexandria, Virginia, 1984.

Chapters 2 & 3

The passage on the pecan and the passage on the Dust Bowl are based on information in *Plant Science* by Janick, Schery, Woods & Ruttan, W.H. Freeman and Company, San Francisco, 1981.

Chapter 5

The passage on laughter is based on information in *Psychology* by Carole Wade & Carol Tavris, Harper & Row Publishers, Inc., New York, 1990. The passage on bird calls is based on information in *The Audubon Society Pocket Guides,* Ann H. Whitman, Editor, Alfred A. Knopf, New York, 1991.

Chapter 10

The passage on the leaf fish is based on information in *Animals and their Colors* by M. & P. Fogden, Crown Publishers, Inc., New York, 1974.

Chapter 12

The passage on Sally Ride is based on information in *American Biographies* by Henry I. Christ, Globe Book Company, New York, 1987.

Chapter 13

The passages in this section are based on information in the *Kids' World Almanac of History* by Deborah G. Felder, Pharos Books, New York, 1991.

CHAPTER 1

Words in Context

Introduction

At some point there may be a word you do not know the meaning of, and there may be no prefix or root to help you. In this case, you must look at the context of the word.

The context of a word is the setting in which the word occurs in speech or in writing. Since you normally learn words by hearing or seeing them in contexts, developing this ability will help you to learn more words.

The following readings include exercises for words in context. With the exception of the last three selections, these passages are lower in overall difficulty than the reading passages you will find in the TOEFL® since the aim of this book is to teach vocabulary.

STRATEGIES

- When looking for clues to the meaning of a word in context, one of the following types of contextual clues will help you:

  1. *Straight definitions*   In some cases where there is an unusual word, a definition of the word is given close by. Try to understand the definition and apply it to the word in context.

  2. *Paraphrases or synonyms*   Look for the possibility of another word or phrase in the context that has the same meaning.

  3. *Implied meaning*   In some contexts direct clues are not given but just implied. In this case you must think about the context and guess what the meaning of the word can be. Even if you cannot determine its exact meaning, you will be able to determine its general meaning.

- Every time you read, practice looking for contextual clues. This will encourage you to analyze the meaning of what you read, and will also train you to think about words and their meanings.

Biology Reading

Read the following passage.

Otters belong to another group of animals, the mustelids. This word comes from the Latin, and means "weasel." Other members of this family of animals include weasels, skunks, and badgers. They are all short-legged, have thick coats of **fur** and sharp, tearing teeth, and are **carnivorous** or meat-eating **mammals**.

Otters love water, and their **webbed** feet, thick tails, and **dense** fur make them well-suited for life in the water. Two kinds of otters are found in and around North America. One is a fresh-water otter; the other is a sea otter.

The home of the fresh-water otter is usually a hole dug into the bank of a stream or lake. The hole leads to a **den** lined with leaves. Here, the young, usually two or three, are born in late winter or early spring. Before the young can swim, the mother sometimes carries them about on her back in the water and feeds them milk.

But the young learn very quickly to swim themselves. Their parents teach them **to dive** and to catch the fish on which they feed. Soon the **cubs** are able to stay underwater for as long as four minutes.

Sea otters are larger and heavier than fresh-water otters. Their thick fur is dark brown with white at the tips and has a **frosted** appearance. They have white **whiskers** from which they get the nickname, the "old men of the sea."

 EXERCISE 1

Working Out the Meaning

Find the words below in the passage. Try to guess the meaning of the words from the passage. Circle the correct answer.

EXAMPLE:

1. fur

   a. thick hair on the body of an animal

   b. hard skin on the body of an animal

In the passage the words "thick coats" are close to the word "fur." A coat is usually made of animal hair, not "hard skin"; therefore, the correct answer is (a).

2. carnivorous

   a. meat-eating

   b. plant-eating

3. mammals

   a. animals that lay eggs

   b. animals that give milk

4. webbed

   a. with skin between the toes

   b. with long nails on the toes

5. dense

   a. thin

   b. thick

6. den

   a. home of a meat-eating
      animal

   b. dead animal used for food

7. to dive

   a. run quickly

   b. jump into the water

8. cubs
   a. the young of the otter
   b. the parents

9. frosted
   a. blue-colored
   b. as if covered with ice

10. whiskers
   a. long ears of an animal
   b. long hairs near the mouth

EXERCISE 2

Dictionary Work

A. Where do these animals live? Match the animal with its home. You may use the same home more than once.

den	hive	web	nest
stable	sty	burrow	

1. otter   _____

2. rabbit   _____

3. bee   _____

4. lion   _____

5. spider   _____

6. pig   _____

7. horse   _____

8. bird   _____

B. List other animals and their homes.

EXERCISE 3

What is the name for the animal's baby? Match the animals on the left with the names of their young on the right. You may use the name of the young more than once.

_____ 1. otter

_____ 2. goat

_____ 3. cow

_____ 4. cat

_____ 5. dog

_____ 6. horse

_____ 7. lion

_____ 8. deer

a. puppy

b. cub

c. kitten

d. foal

e. kid

f. fawn

g. calf

Science Reading (1)

Read the following passage.

The shooting star that **streaks** across the sky is a tiny **particle** or piece of matter from outer space. When the particle enters the earth's atmosphere, **friction** with the air causes it to **glow** white hot and then turn to gas. Most of these particles, or meteors, are smaller than a **grain** of rice.

Comets move around the sun and have a very bright head and a long tail. Many meteors seem to be **fragments** of comets that **crashed** into one another. Other meteors are tiny particles from the tails of comets. Some meteors are iron and some are stone.

Once in a while, an extra bright meteor, or fireball, appears. Fireballs can sometimes be seen during the day and may even be as bright as the full moon. Some meteors survive their fall through the Earth's atmosphere and **land** on the ground. These are called meteorites, and are usually cool enough to touch when they land.

 EXERCISE 1

Working Out the Meaning

Find the words below in the passage. Try to guess the meaning of the words from the passage. Circle the correct answer.

1. streak
   a. move very fast
   b. move slowly

2. particle
   a. piece of matter
   b. piece of space

3. friction
   a. appearance
   b. rapid movement

4. grain
   a. seed
   b. field

5. glow
   a. give out cold
   b. give out light

6. fragments
   a. small pieces
   b. ice pieces

7. crashed
   a. hit violently
   b. mix slowly

8. land
   a. go out
   b. come down

 EXERCISE 2

One word in each group does not belong. Find the word.

1. hot glow cool grain

2. particle fragment comet grain

3. meteor comet fireball sky

4. space moon star land

EXERCISE 3

Dictionary Work

The following words represent small pieces or quantities. Match the word and the object it goes with.

grain	fragment	trace	blade
speck	flake	breath	item

1. _____ of sand

2. _____ of grass

3. _____ of dust

4. _____ of fresh air

5. _____ of snow

6. _____ of news

7. _____ of a vase

8. _____ of poison

EXERCISE 4

Put the following words in order of size from the smallest to the largest.

earth	star	meteor	universe
solar system	galaxy		

1. _____

2. _____

3. _____

4. _____

5. _____

6. _____

Reading about People

Read the following passage.

Horace Mann has been called the "Father of Public Education" because of the great educational **reforms** he started in American public schools.

He was born in 1796 in Massachusetts. Mann gave up a **promising** career as a lawyer to become the first superintendent of education for Massachusetts in 1837. For twelve years he **pleaded**, argued, and **lectured** the state government to improve the schools.

Mann was a **dedicated** reformer. He even spent his vacations visiting schools around the country. Mann believed the **effort** was worth the price. In his opinion a democratic republic needed well-educated citizens.

During his **term** as superintendent, education made important **strides** in Massachusetts. He doubled teachers' salaries, and raised the minimum time children must attend school to six months a year. He improved the quality of teaching by starting new training schools for teachers.

 EXERCISE **1**

Working Out the Meaning

Find the words in the passage. Try to guess the meaning of the words from the passage. Circle the correct answer.

1. reforms
   a. improvements
   b. arrangements

2. promising
   a. untrustworthy
   b. hopefully successful

3. pleaded
   a. implored
   b. understood

4. lectured
   a. taught
   b. warned

5. dedicated
   a. devoted
   b. educated

6. effort
   a. chance
   b. hard work

7. term
   a. improvement
   b. period of time

8. strides
   a. steps forward
   b. arguments

 EXERCISE **2**

Dictionary Work—Time Periods

A. Look up the words below and then complete the sentences.

period	spell	term	semester	era
span	decade	an epoch	age	

1. The _____ of space exploration started in the 1960s.

   a. period   b. era   c. spell

2. The computer _____ has helped to improve global communication.

   a. age   b. term   c. span

3. The discovery of the Americas began _____ of adventure.

   a. a semester   b. a spell   c. an epoch

4. From 1990 to the year 2000 is the last _____ of the 20th century.

   a. epoch   b. decade   c. span

5. Many colleges in the United States run on _____ system.

   a. a decade   b. an era   c. a semester

6. The president of the United States can only serve two _____ of four years.

   a. epochs   b. terms   c. age

7. The Civil War was the climax of a very important _____ in the growth of the United States of America.

   a. period   b. spell   c. age

8. The northern part of the country experienced a very cold _____ in the winter of 1993.

   a. term   b. spell   c. era

9. The Pony Express lasted for a _____ of 18 months.

   a. term   b. spell   c. span

B. List any other words you know for periods of time.

 EXERCISE 3

One word in each group does not belong. Find the word.

1. oppose   resist   start   rebel
2. protest   demonstrate   riot   improve
3. plead   urge   teach   request

Reading on Social Science

Read the following passage.

The Shoshone were a group of Indian tribes who lived in the western plains of Wyoming, Utah, Nevada, and Idaho. Life in this almost **arid**, desertlike region was difficult. The Shoshone lived by hunting small animals and **gathering** nuts, fruits, and seeds. Most Shoshone lived together in small family groups. An older person in each group was the leader. Each group was known to the others by the type of food that was **plentiful** in its **particular** region. The "Sheep Eaters" and "Seed Eaters" were two such groups.

In the 1700s the Shoshone received guns from the Spanish. Some of them became hunters like their neighbors, the **nomadic** Comanche tribe.

Perhaps the most famous member of the Shoshone tribe was Sacagawea, the woman who **accompanied** Merriwether Lewis and William Clark on their **expedition** across the West.

Today, more than 10,000 Shoshone Indians live on or near reservations in the western United States. Most of them are ranchers, farmers, and **laborers**.

 EXERCISE 1

Working Out the Meaning

Find the words in the passage. Try to guess the meaning of the words from the passage. Circle the correct answer.

1. arid
   a. dry
   b. wet

2. gathering
   a. scattering
   b. collecting

3. plentiful
   a. scarce
   b. abundant

4. particular
   a. special
   b. general

5. nomadic
   a. wandering
   b. farming

6. accompanied
   a. settled with
   b. went with

7. expedition
   a. journey
   b. trade

8. laborers
   a. traders
   b. workers

 EXERCISE 2

Dictionary Work

A. Look up the adjectives below. Put the adjectives under the two headings *dry / not dry*.

damp	arid	dessicated	humid	baked
parched	saturated	immersed	soaked	moist

Dry	*Not Dry*
_____	_____
_____	_____
_____	_____
_____	_____
_____	_____

B.   Add your own words under each heading.

 EXERCISE 3

Synonyms and Antonyms

List as many synonyms of *plentiful* and of its antonym *scarce* as you can.

	Synonyms	*Antonyms*
1.	plentiful	scarce
2.	_____	_____
3.	_____	_____
4.	_____	_____
5.	_____	_____

EXERCISE 4

One word in each group does not belong. Find the word.

1.   expedition   journey   voyage   reservation
2.   ranchers   farmers   laborers   neighbors
3.   gathering   collecting   hunting   picking
4.   wanderer   tribe   traveler   nomad

History Reading

Read the following passage.

Sequoya was a Cherokee Indian who invented an alphabet that **enabled** his people to read and write their own language.

Sequoya was born in Tennessee in 1770, the son of an Indian mother and a white father. Sequoya was first a hunter, but after a hunting accident he became a trader. Sequoya had no education, but he knew that reading and writing were important. He began to work on an alphabet for the Cherokee language. In 1823, after 12 years of work, his alphabet was ready. It consisted of symbols for 85 sounds that **make up** the Cherokee language.

Within a few months thousands of Cherokees learned to read and write using the new alphabet. Soon a Cherokee newspaper called the *Phoenix* was being published. Its **columns** carried news in both English and Cherokee.

Sequoya became a teacher and moved to Oklahoma where he continued to teach the alphabet. The **huge** sequoia trees, known for their great size, that grow in California are named in his memory and **honor**.

 EXERCISE 1

Working Out the Meaning

Find the words below in the passage. Try to guess the meaning of the words from the passage. Circle the correct answer.

1. enabled
    a. let
    b. made

2. make up
    a. color
    b. comprise

3. columns
    a. newspaper articles
    b. newspaper sellers

4. huge
    a. immense
    b. minuscule

5. honor
    a. courage
    b. recognition

 EXERCISE 2

Dictionary Work

One word in each group does not mean *big*. Find the word.

1. bulky   immense   dwarf
2. vast   infinitesimal   colossal
3. monumental   minute   substantial
4. considerable   huge   memorial

EXERCISE 3

A. Where do you find these? Put the words below under the correct heading.

column	bibliography	article
editorial	headline	appendix
index	biography	glossary

Newspaper   *Book*

_____   _____

_____   _____

_____   _____

_____   _____

_____   _____

B. Add other words under each heading.

EXERCISE 4

Give synonyms for the following phrasal verbs. You may write more than one synonym.

1. make up   = comprise_____

2. set up   = establish_____

3. put up   = _____

4. take place   = _____

5. tie up   = _____

6. pick up   = _____

Reading on Earthquakes

Read the following passage.

The people of Mexico City felt the ground shake several times on September 19–20, 1985. Each **tremor** was a little stronger than the one before. A **rumbling** sound seemed to approach the city. The rumble increased to a **roar**, as if a huge train were rushing through a tunnel under the streets. The ground rose and fell in waves. After the main shocks came a brief **pause**, followed by renewed shaking, the aftershock.

People were thrown off their feet by the shaking of the earth. Apartment buildings crumbled into **heaps**. Many buildings in Mexico's capital were **damaged**. Thousands of persons were hurt or killed by falling buildings.

 EXERCISE 1

Working Out the Meaning

Find the words in the passage. Try to guess the meaning of the words from the passage. Circle the correct answer.

1. tremor
   a. shake
   b. wave

2. rumbling
   a. a deep sound
   b. a loud sound

3. roar
   a. soft sound
   b. loud sound

4. pause
   a. stop
   b. shake

5. heaps
   a. piles
   b. shakes

6. damaged
   a. cracked
   b. destroyed

 EXERCISE 2

Dictionary Work

A. Look up the words below that mean *damage / destroy*. Then put them under the headings they go with. You may use the same word more than once.

hurt	impair	injure	spoil
harm	mar	damage	destroy

Feelings	*Your Leg*	*Your Reputation*
_____	_____	_____
_____	_____	_____
_____	_____	_____
_____	_____	_____

A Painting	*The Environment*	*Your Health*
_____	_____	_____
_____	_____	_____
_____	_____	_____
_____	_____	_____

B. Add your own words for *destroy / damage* under the headings. You can start a new heading.

EXERCISE 3

A. Work alone or with a partner. Look up the words for the *types of sound* given below. Put each under one of the headings.

roar	rumble	rattle	crack	hum
rustle	squeak	bang	slam	murmur

Continuous Sound   *Single Sound*

_____   _____

_____   _____

_____   _____

_____   _____

_____   _____

B. Add more sounds under each heading.

EXERCISE 4

Choose the sound that is louder.

1. a. hum
   b. rumble

2. a. rustle
   b. rattle

3. a. roar
   b. rumble

4. a. crack
   b. slam

5. a. murmur
   b. rumble

6. a. bang
   b. squeak

EXERCISE 5

Choose the correct sound to complete the sentence.

1. The bees are _____ around the flowers.

   a. humming   b. squeaking

2. The mouse _____.

   a. cracked   b. squeaked

3. The wind _____ the door shut.

   a. slammed   b. roared

4. The leaves _____ in the wind.

   a. rattled   b. rustled

5. The thunder _____ in the distance.

   a. slammed   b. rumbled

 EXERCISE 6

A. Match the animal with the sound it makes.

_____ 1. a bee   a. hisses

_____ 2. a bird   b. buzzes

_____ 3. a snake   c. bleats

_____ 4. a sheep   d. twitters

_____ 5. a lion   e. croaks

_____ 6. a frog   f. roars

B. Write three more animals and the sound they make.

Science Reading (2)

Read the following passage.

Rubber can be made from latex, the **sap** of a rubber tree. Rubber can also be made **synthetically** by combining the chemical **elements** carbon and hydrogen. Synthetic substances are often artificial **imitations** of natural substances. A synthetic that is exactly like a natural substance is made up of the same elements as the natural substance. For example, a natural diamond is made up of carbon atoms, but the atoms are arranged in a certain **pattern**. A synthetic diamond is also made up of carbon atoms, but the atoms are arranged in a pattern by people. Nevertheless, the synthetic diamond is still a real diamond. However, there are imitation diamonds made of the chemical compound titanium dioxide. These diamonds are not synthetic. They are **fake** diamonds because they are not made of up the same chemical elements as natural diamonds.

A synthetic product may be better than a natural substance. For example, synthetic rubber is better than natural rubber for some uses because it can be made stronger.

 EXERCISE 1

Working Out the Meaning

Find the words in the passage. Try to guess the meaning of the words from the passage. Circle the correct answer.

1. sap
   a. chemical
   b. juice

2. synthetically
   a. artificially
   b. naturally

3. elements
   a. basic substances
   b. products

4. imitations
   a. chemicals
   b. copies

5. pattern
   a. substance
   b. arrangement

6. fake
   a. false
   b. natural

 EXERCISE 2

Dictionary Work—"Not real"

A. The words *fake, false, counterfeit, phony,* and *artificial* all mean "not real." Put the words below under the correct heading. You may use the same word more than once.

smile	flowers	sweetener	address
diamonds	picture	impression	alarm
money	letters	statement	teeth

16

False	Fake	Counterfeit
_____	_____	_____
_____	_____	_____
_____	_____	_____
_____	_____	_____
_____	_____	_____

Phony	Artificial
_____	_____
_____	_____
_____	_____
_____	_____
_____	_____

B. Add your own words under each heading. You can start a new heading.

EXERCISE 3

Liquids

EXAMPLE

Sap = liquid in a plant

Juice = liquid in a fruit or vegetable

Write the definitions of these words:

1. secretion = _____

2. resin = _____

3. extract = _____

4. fluid = _____

EXERCISE 4

One word in each group does not belong. Find the word.

1. arrangement   order   copy

2. artificial   compound   counterfeit

3. a product   a form of matter   a basic substance

Science Reading (3)

Read the following passage.

A **satellite** is a body that moves in an **orbit** about a larger body. Our moon is a satellite of Earth. Earth and the eight other planets are satellites of the sun. These are natural satellites. The Earth has many artificial satellites too. Most artificial satellites are used for research and communication.

Communication satellites have had the greatest effect on our daily lives. They have made it possible for **live** radio and television **broadcasts** to be carried around the world.

A communication satellite is like a big mirror for radio and television signals. A television signal is sent from Japan high into space and hits the communication satellite. It **bounces off** the satellite and is directed toward the United States, where it is picked up by television stations and **relayed** to millions of viewers at home.

 EXERCISE 1

Working Out the Meaning

Find the words in the passage. Try to guess the meaning of the words from the passage. Circle the correct answer.

1. satellite
   a. a body that moves
   b. a body that moves around a larger body

2. an orbit
   a. a planet
   b. a path

3. live
   a. seen as it happens
   b. recorded

4. broadcasts
   a. stations
   b. presentations

5. bounces off
   a. passes by
   b. springs back from

6. relayed
   a. transmitted
   b. stopped

 EXERCISE 2

One word or word phrase in each group does not belong. Find the word.

1. carry around   relay   hit   transmit
2. broadcast   space   viewers   television
3. planet   television   satellite   earth
4. orbit   communication   radio   television

EXERCISE 3

Dictionary Work

The following words indicate "paths." Choose the appropriate word to complete the sentences.

orbit	trail	circuit	course

1. The hunter followed the animal's _____.

2. The satellite went out of its _____ and lost contact with earth.

3. After the flood, the _____ of the river changed.

4. The movie was shown only on closed _____ television.

 EXERCISE 4

List as many synonyms of *transmit* and of its antonym *pick up* as you can.

Synonyms	*Antonyms*
1. transmit	pick up
2. send out	_____
3. _____	_____
4. _____	_____
5. _____	_____
6. _____	_____

Reading on Literature

Read the following passage.

The three major types of poetry are narrative, lyric, and dramatic. **Narrative** poetry tells a story. It includes **epic** poems, which are long **tales** or stories usually taken from history, or legends about brave or **heroic** acts.

The ballad is another kind of narrative poem. It is shorter and is often sung. Lyric poetry tells the poet's own feelings and thoughts. Lyric poems were once sung to the musical accompaniment of a stringed instrument called a lyre, after which the poetry was named.

Dramatic poetry has **characters** who tell a story through **dialogue**, just as a play does. Some plays, such as those of Shakespeare, are written almost entirely in **verse** or poetry.

 EXERCISE **1**

Working Out the Meaning

Find the words in the passage. Try to guess the meaning of the words from the passage. Circle the correct answer.

1. narrative
   a. poetry
   b. story

2. epic
   a. a short story
   b. a long poem

3. tales
   a. stories
   b. poems

4. heroic
   a. something from history
   b. something brave

5. characters
   a. poems
   b. people

6. dialogue
   a. conversation
   b. thoughts

7. verse
   a. poetry
   b. songs

 EXERCISE **2**

Dictionary Work

Look up the words below and then complete the sentences.

a chronicle	verse	dialogue	prose	a nursery rhyme
a rhyme	a poet	a lyric	an epic	a monologue

1. A long story full of brave actions is _____.
2. A person who writes poems is _____.
3. A story or real events over a period of time in the order in which they happened is

    _____.

4. A short story that is often sung is _____ poem.
5. Shakespeare's plays are written in _____.
6. Written language, not poetry, as in books or newspapers is called _____.
7. A word or line which ends with the same sound as another as in "day" and "way" is

    _____.

8. A short well-known song or poem for young children is _____.
9. A long speech or poem spoken by one person is _____.
10. A written conversation in a book or play is _____.

EXERCISE 3

One word in each group does not belong. Find the word.

1. story   tale   anecdote   abridgement
2. fearless   heroic   accomplished   brave
3. personage   figure   accompaniment   character
4. legend   fable   history   myth

Archeology Reading

Read the following passage.

Ancient peoples often built cities on top of older **decayed** ones. Many layers, called **strata**, made at different times may be in one **site,** underneath each other. Archeologists very carefully dig down through the layers, keeping **accurate** records all the while. It is important that archeologists record exactly where an object was found, and what other objects were found near it, in order to know the **context** of a find. Then they can build a sequence of events in the correct order. If a single object is removed, this valuable evidence of the order in which objects were buried will be destroyed.

Archeologists **seek** the help of other experts to discover all they can about an object. Botanists identify plants from which **preserved** pollen grains or seeds originally came. Zoologists can do the same from animal **remains**.

 EXERCISE 1

Working Out the Meaning

Find the words in the passage. Try to guess the meaning of the words from the passage. Circle the correct answer.

1. decayed
   a. ruined
   b. removed

2. strata
   a. times
   b. layers

3. site
   a. place
   b. animal

4. accurate
   a. original
   b. precise

5. context
   a. environment
   b. reading

6. seek
   a. dig
   b. try to find

7. preserved
   a. carefully kept
   b. destroyed

8. remains
   a. corpses
   b. seeds

 EXERCISE 2

Dictionary Work

Look up the words below. Then match the words in *Column A* with the group they are connected to in *Column B*. You may use one word more than once.

Column A	Column B
__C__ 1. remnants	a. food
_____ 2. remains	b. money
_____ 3. leftovers	c. clothes

_____ 4. remainder   d. animals

_____ 5. relics   e. destroyed buildings

_____ 6. residual   f. old times, objects

                              g. water

EXERCISE 3

Synonyms and Antonyms

List as many synonyms of *accurate* and of its antonym *incorrect* as you can.

	Synonyms	Antonyms
1.	accurate	incorrect
2.	exact	
3.		
4.		
5.		
6.		

EXERCISE 4

One word in each group does not belong. Find the word.

1. site   place   country

2. position   locality   building

3. situation   city   spot

4. scene   point   botanist

EXERCISE 5

Decay and Rot

To decay = to rot.
To rot = to decay only for organic matter (living things).

Put the following words under the correct heading.

teeth	flesh	apples	a statue	trees
society	standards	buildings	tomatoes	wood

23

Decay	Rot
buildings	apples
_____	_____
_____	_____
_____	_____
_____	_____

 EXERCISE **6**

Preserve

We can *preserve* things in many ways. Can you add to the list below?

1. To dehydrate—to remove water from _____

2. To pickle—to put in vinegar and salt water _____

3. _____

4. _____

5. _____

Sample TOEFL® Tests

The following three passages are similar to those found in the Reading Section of the TOEFL® test.

Sample Test 1

Anna Mary Robertson Moses, known as "Grandma" Moses, began to paint in 1938 at the age of 78, after giving up embroidery due to an arthritic condition. Two years later her first exhibition was held and this 80-year-old self-taught artist experienced sudden and dramatic success. Moses had spent her life first as a hired girl and later as the wife of a farmer, and her paintings **reflected** the peace and simplicity of the country life she had always known. Scenes such as harvesting, collecting sap for maple syrup, county fairs and landscapes in all seasons from snow-covered villages to summer fields, were the pleasant subjects she chose for her work.

People were attracted to Moses' appealing subjects and her **renditions** of the seasons and landscapes of her native New York State. However they were just as moved by the story of this gifted **octogenarian** who with no formal training went from complete **obscurity** to world fame in a handful of years, and who opened up for them a **rustic** world of tranquility and simple pleasure they **yearned** to enjoy.

EXERCISE 1

Circle the letter of the correct answer.

1. Which of the following words could best be substituted for "reflected"?
   (A) Polished
   (B) Caught
   (C) Recognized
   (D) Copied

2. The word "renditions" could best be replaced by which of the following?
   (A) Depictions
   (B) Recollections
   (C) Translations
   (D) Patterns

3. The word "octogenarian" could best be replaced by which of the following?
   (A) Person in his seventies
   (B) Person in his nineties
   (C) Person in his eighties
   (D) Person who has eight talents

4. The word "obscurity" could best be replaced by which of the following?
   (A) Uncertainty
   (B) Incomprehensibility
   (C) Poverty
   (D) Unknown

5. Which of the following words could best be substituted for "rustic"?
   (A) Degenerate
   (B) Country
   (C) Rusted
   (D) Contemporary

6. The word "yearned" could best be replaced by which of the following?
   (A) Longed
   (B) Appeared
   (C) Contemplated
   (D) Imagined

EXERCISE 2

Dictionary Work

Look at the following prefixes:

uni-, mono-: one	*duo-, bi-*: two	*tri-*: three
quad-, quart-: four	*pent-, quin-*: five	*sex-*: six
sept-: seven	*oct-*: eight	*non-*: nine
dec-: ten	*cent-*: hundred	

A. Use your dictionary to complete the sentences below using the prefixes above.

1. A flag with three colors is a _____ flag.

2. Five children born at the same time are _____.

3. A bicycle with one wheel is a _____.

4. One hundred years is a _____.

5. A shape with five sides is a _____.

6. A person who is in his/her sixties is a _____.

7. A ten-event athletic contest is called _____.

8. Something with one unvaried sound is _____.

9. A magazine that appears twice a month is _____.

10. To make something four times as great is to _____ it.

B. Write one other word that can be made with each of the prefixes above.

Sample Test 2

In the brutal high-desert environment of California's White Mountains, the bristlecone pines, their bare and twisted frames looking more dead than alive, preside over an **eerie** rock-**strewn** landscape. Capable of enduring bitter cold, **ceaseless** wind and extreme drought, the bristlecones are the oldest living things on earth, enduring for more than 4,000 years. In many cases, much of the tree's wood is dead, but live branches **persistently** grow from trunks and limbs. Ironically, for all their ability to exist under such harsh conditions, the bristlecone pine could not exist in another environment, having lost its ability to produce hardier **strains** that could compete with other trees and vegetation. In all probability, these trees will never extend their **range**, and are essentially at the end of their evolutionary development.

 EXERCISE 1

Circle the letter of the correct answer.

1. Which of the following words could best be substituted for "eerie"?
   - (A) Irritating
   - (B) Ghostly
   - (C) Artificial
   - (D) Faraway

2. The word "strewn" could best be replaced by which of the following?
   - (A) Damaged
   - (B) Looking
   - (C) Scattered
   - (D) Shaped

3. The word "ceaseless" could best be replaced by which of the following?
   - (A) Continual
   - (B) Corrosive
   - (C) Potent
   - (D) Infinite

4. The word "persistently" could best be replaced by which of the following?
   - (A) Perilously
   - (B) Imaginatively
   - (C) Tenaciously
   - (D) Harmoniously

5. The word "strains" could best be replaced by which of the following?
   - (A) Traces
   - (B) Varieties
   - (C) Remnants
   - (D) Projections

6. Which of the following words could best be substituted for "range"?

(A) Length   (B) Sphere

(C) Wilderness   (D) Scope

EXERCISE 2

The word "rock-strewn" is a compound adjective. What other compounds (nouns and adjectives) can you make with the words in bold print?

EXAMPLE

Rock

rock-bottom   igneous rock

| molten | fall | salt | crystal | weed |
| rose | oil | bound | candy | pervious |

Tree

| genealogical | house | line | frog |
| farm | banana | vascular | |

Now add your own words to make more compounds.

Make as many compound nouns and adjectives as possible with the words "environment" and "landscape."

Environment   *Landscape*

_____   _____

_____   _____

_____   _____

_____   _____

_____   _____

Sample Test 3

Art as a **reflection** of human social history is clearly illustrated in the Pop Art style of the 1960s. In the post–World War II years, Americans were **inundated** with material goods from cars to kitchen appliances. The manufactured products and ready-made experiences with which Americans surrounded themselves were part of a modern era **epitomized** by TV screens, **slick** magazines, fast food and air-conditioned cars. Dramatic cultural changes occurred in American life, which **profoundly** affected American painting, in style as well as content.

The ever-multiplying images of the new consumer society became the subjects of Pop (for popular) Art, represented in paintings by Andy Warhol, Roy Lichtenstein, Claes Oldenburg, and James Rosenquist. These artists not only used standardized, mass-produced goods as the subjects of their paintings but came as close as they could to the containers in which these products were packaged. Andy Warhol's *One Hundred Campbell's Soup Cans* (1962), Roy Lichtenstein's *Whaam!* (1963), and James Rosenquist's *F-111* (1965) are examples of the artists' use of ordinary objects, presented as they appear, as subjects for painting. In doing so, these Pop artists were presenting a "new realism," or reflection, of **contemporary** life in America.

 EXERCISE 1

Circle the letter of the correct answer.

1. The word "reflection" could best be replaced by which of the following?

    (A) Imagination   (B) Contemplation

    (C) Representation   (D) Absorption

2. Which of the following words could best be substituted for "inundated"?

    (A) Ruined   (B) Beaten

    (C) Embarrassed   (D) Overwhelmed

3. The word "epitomized" could best be replaced by which of the following?

    (A) Typified   (B) Systemized

    (C) Supervised   (D) Glorified

4. The word "slick" could best be replaced by which of the following?

    (A) Smooth   (B) Glossy

    (C) Monotonous   (D) Educational

5. Which of the following words could best be substituted for "profoundly"?

    (A) Deeply   (B) Mysteriously

    (C) Partially   (D) Scientifically

6. The word "contemporary" could best be replaced by which of the following?

    (A) Fashionable   (B) Advanced

    (C) Untraditional   (D) Present-day

EXERCISE 2

A. Which of the following words are NOT related to art? Look up the words in a dictionary and check the ones not related to art.

_____ 1. Impressionism   _____ 2. Silurian

_____ 3. Expressionism   _____ 4. Carboniferous

_____ 5. Surrealist   _____ 6. Cretaceous

_____ 7. Cubism   _____ 8. Triassic

B. What are the other words related to?

EXERCISE 3

Give antonyms for these words:

1. inundated   _____

2. slick   _____

3. contemporary   _____

4. profoundly   _____

5. to present (v)   _____

CHAPTER 2

Theme Grouping:
Living Things

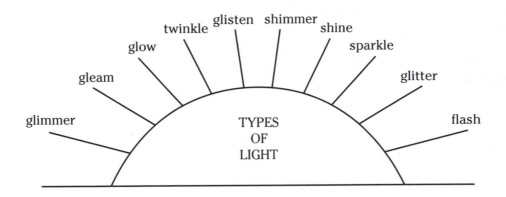

Introduction

Another way of building your vocabulary is by looking at words with similar meanings in themes. For example, if we take the theme "Types of Light," we find there are several words that mean "to shine" but each is slightly different in intensity and use. The word "glisten" means "to shine," but is often associated with things that are wet, whereas the word "twinkle" implies the light is unsteady and is often associated with the stars or a person's eye.

In this section there are different themes with exercises that accompany them. Since only a certain number of themes can be covered in this book, it is suggested that you start to make your own themes with the use of a dictionary in order to continue to build your vocabulary.

Reading Practice

Read the following passage.

The pecan was highly regarded as a wild nut tree by the **settlers** in what are now the border states to Mexico and the upper South of the United States. Today, they are grown chiefly in Georgia and Alabama where they are harvested from wild and **seedling** trees. They are also grown in Louisiana, Texas, and Oklahoma. There is little growing of the pecan outside the United States, although it has been successfully introduced to Australia and China.

The pecan has an outer leathery **husk** that splits open when mature to reveal an inner **shell** that surrounds the two **kernels**. Harvest is by picking the nuts from fallen fruits. Sometimes the fruits are knocked from the trees with long poles, but since a mature pecan tree is so large, mechanical harvesting is not possible. The nuts are dried for a few weeks, and they are ready for eating without roasting or other treatment.

 EXERCISE 1

Work with a partner, with a group, or alone to answer the following questions. Write or say the answers.

1. Who regarded the pecan highly?

Task

What words do you know for people living in a country? Are these people settlers? Give reasons.

2. What kinds of trees are pecans harvested from?

Task

What do plants grow from? Describe the life of a plant.

3. What does a pecan nut have on the outside?

Task

What other fruits or nuts do you know that have a dry outer shell?

4. What surrounds the two kernels?

Task

Name three things that have shells. What fruits or nuts have an inside part or a kernel?

Conversation Practice

Read the following conversation.

Tom: Betty, I'd like you to meet my friend, Sonja. She's an **immigrant** from Russia.
Betty: I'm pleased to meet you, Sonja. As you know, I'm a colleague of Tom's.
Sonja: Oh, yes. Tom has told me so much about you.
Betty: Are you enjoying Southern California?
Sonja: Yes, very much. As a matter of fact, I already feel like a **native**. I've even learned to surf.

31

Betty:	Wonderful! But what is that you're eating? It certainly isn't a California orange.
Sonja:	No, it's a pomegranate. Would you like to try one?
Betty:	Why, yes, thank you.
Sonja:	You can't eat the **rind**, naturally, just the **flesh** around the **seeds**. It's very sweet. I'm sure you'll like it.
Betty:	Thank you, Sonja. That's very nice of you. In return, I'll bring you some **blooms** from my rose garden.
Sonja:	Thank you. I'd like that. I must be going now. See you tomorrow.

EXERCISE 2

Work with a partner, with a group, or alone to answer the following questions.

1. Is Sonja a tourist from Russia?

Task

What do you think is the difference between a tourist and an immigrant?

2. How does Betty know Tom?

Task

What other words for friends do you know?

3. How does Sonja feel about living in Southern California?

Task

What is typical of a native of your country? Name some native fruits or plants of your country.

4. What can you and can't you eat on a pomegranate?

Task

Name some other fruits with a rind, flesh, and seeds.

5. What will Betty bring Sonja?

Task

Name three plants with blooms.

STRATEGIES

- New vocabulary items are best learned with a group of words associated with a theme. It is easier to understand and remember a word such as "bud" when it is connected to a plant, because you can distinguish it from "blossom" and "seedling," than to learn these words in isolation.

- You may know or recognize some of the words in each theme. This will help you remember the new words that you do not know.

- Some words come under the same general meaning but differ slightly in meaning and use. For example, "to sparkle" and "to glow" both mean "to shine" but their meaning is slightly different. "To sparkle" means to give small flashes of light, whereas "to glow" means to give a soft light or heat. Use associations to remember the difference in meaning. For example,

"sparkle" — diamonds, glass, water

"glow" — soft, warm light of a fire

- Attach new words to one basic word that you already know. Create your own themes. Here are some suggestions: Seeing and Looking, Rough and Not Rough, Good and Not Good, Damage and Destroy.

A. Types of Inhabitants

inhabitant	dweller	resident
pioneer	settler	native
colonist	immigrant	

1. **inhabitant** = a person or animal that lives in one place, usually a country or a region for a very long time.

    Ex. The only human inhabitants of the Gobi desert are some nomadic tribes.

2. **dweller** = a person or animal that lives in a named place such as a cave, tree, or a city.

    Ex. Most city dwellers get used to the high levels of noise.

3. **resident** = a person or animal that lives in a place, usually a house, but is not a visitor. It is also used for a person who lives permanently in a particular country or state.

    Ex. Most of the residents of this neighborhood park their cars on the street.

4. **pioneer** = a person who is one of the first to come to an unknown land, and then is followed by others. A person who is the first to discover something which opens the way to others.

    Ex. The Wright brothers were pioneers in aviation.

5. **native** = used of a person, plant, or animal when you refer to the place of its origin.

    Ex. The Koala bear is a native of Australia.

6. **settler** = a person who is one of the first of a group to put their roots down in a new country.

    Ex. The first settlers in America were the Pilgrims who came from England.

7. **colonist** = a person who is one of a group of settlers from the same country or under the control of the same country.

    Ex. The early colonists faced many hardships in a new land.

8. **immigrant** = a person who comes to a country to make a new home there. The first immigrants are called settlers.

    Ex. Alexander Graham Bell, the inventor of the telephone, was an immigrant who came to America from Scotland.

EXERCISE 1

Circle T if the sentence is TRUE and F if the sentence is FALSE.

1. A pioneer usually lives in a hotel or a house.   T   F
2. The aborigines, a group of people who always lived in Australia,
   are immigrants to Australia.   T   F
3. A native Californian is a person who was born in California.   T   F
4. A colonist is a person who lives in a cave or tree.   T   F
5. Cave dwellers are usually called colonists.   T   F
6. A resident is a person who comes to a new country to settle and live there.   T   F
7. The most commonly known inhabitant of the North Pole is the polar bear.   T   F
8. European settlers came to live in America in the 17th century.   T   F

EXERCISE 2

Complete the sentences with the correct answer.

1. The Dutch who went and lived in South Africa were _____.

   a. colonists   b. natives   c. dwellers

2. The orangutan, a large ape, is a _____ of Sumatra and Borneo.

   a. pioneer   b. native   c. dweller

3. Levi Strauss, the man who invented blue jeans, was _____ to the United States
   from Germany.

   a. an immigrant   b. a settler   c. an inhabitant

4. The native American Indians helped the first _____ from England to survive in a
   new land.

   a. residents   b. inhabitants   c. settlers

5. Dinosaurs were one of the first _____ of the earth.

   a. immigrants   b. inhabitants   c. residents

6. All the _____ of the hotel were evacuated when the fire began.

   a. pioneers   b. settlers   c. residents

7. Cave _____ left drawings on the walls of their caves.

   a. residents   b. dwellers   c. pioneers

8. Yuri Gagarin was a _____ in space travel.

   a. settler   b. native   c. pioneer

B.   The Life of Plants

seedling   sprout   shoot   bud   to bloom   to wilt   to droop   to wither
to blossom

1. **a seedling** = a tiny young plant which has just grown from a seed.

   Ex. Ten days after the seeds were planted, the seedlings appeared.

2. **a sprout** = a new growth from a plant, especially a vegetable.

   Ex. These onions must be old, they have sprouts on them.

3. **a shoot** = a new growth from a plant or a new branch of a tree.

   Ex. After the rose bush was cut back, new shoots started to grow.

4. **a bud** = a flower which has not yet opened, or the beginnings of a leaf.

   Ex. When you buy roses they are usually buds.

5. **to blossom** = to flower, usually used for fruit trees.

   Ex. In the spring, the cherry trees blossom.

6. **to bloom** or **to be in bloom** = to have flowers or to be in flower.

   Ex. The park is beautiful with the roses in bloom.

7. **to wilt** = to become less fresh or weak, or to lose strength.

   Ex. In hot weather most flowers start to wilt because they need water.

8. **to droop** = to hang downwards.

   Ex. It was sad to see the sunflowers drooping towards the ground.

9. **to wither** = to start to dry up and/or become smaller in size.

   Ex. Because there had been no rain for a year, the fruit on the trees started to wilt.

EXERCISE 1

Put the following words in the order of growth of a plant's life. Start from the beginning of a plant's life.

a shoot	a seedling	to wither	a bud
to droop	to bloom	to wilt	

1. _____   2. _____   3. _____

4. _____   5. _____   6. _____

7. _____

 EXERCISE 2

Complete the sentences with the correct answer.

1. When the orange trees are _____ there is a sweet fragrance in the air.

   a. blooming   b. blossoming   c. withering

2. The roses I left in the car yesterday started to _____ after a couple of hours in the heat.

   a. wither   b. blossom   c. wilt

3. That tree has not grown very much in years, but this year there is a new _____ coming out.

   a. shoot   b. bud   c. sprout

4. After you plant your seeds, don't forget to water them every day or you won't see any _____.

   a. blooms   b. seedlings   c. buds

5. The heads of the flowers were _____ after two weeks without water.

   a. blooming   b. wilting   c. drooping

6. If you keep potatoes in a warm and damp place they will grow _____.

   a. sprouts   b. seedlings   c. buds

7. The hills look golden when the gold poppies are in _____.

   a. bud   b. bloom   c. blossom

8. The vines got a strange disease, and the grapes started to _____.

   a. bloom   b. wither   c. blossom

9. When we got the plant, we didn't know that the _____ would open into such beautiful blooms.

   a. sprouts   b. buds   c. shoots

C. Parts of a Fruit or Nut

1. **the seed/stone/pit** = the small hard part of a fruit that can grow into a small plant.

    Ex. Cherries have hard seeds/stones/pits.

2. **the pip** = the small seed of fruit, usually of apples, oranges, lemons, etc. It is sometimes used instead of "pit," "seed," or "stone."

    Ex. When you make orange juice be sure to take the pips out.

3. **the kernel** = the inside part of a fruit stone, a nut, or wheat. It also means the important or central part of something.

    Ex. The pistachio nut has a delicious green kernel.

4. **the peel** = the outer covering of a fruit such as on oranges or apples.

    Ex. You cannot eat a banana with its peel on.

5. **the rind** = the outer covering of certain fruits like oranges, lemons, or melons.

    Ex. Orange rind and lemon rind are often candied or used in marmalade.

6. **the skin** = the general word for the outer covering of a fruit such as the peel, the rind, the husk.

    Ex. If you put tomatoes in boiling water, the skin will come off more easily.

7. **the husk** = the dry outer covering of a fruit, nut, or grain.

    Ex. You remove the husk from corn before eating it.

8. **the flesh** = the soft substance of a fruit.

    Ex. The peach has a soft yellowish flesh.

9. **the shell** = the hard outer covering of a fruit, nut, or egg.

    Ex. Most common nuts like hazelnuts, almonds, and walnuts have shells.

 EXERCISE 1

Circle T if the sentence is TRUE and F if the sentence is FALSE.

1.	The shell is the outer covering of an apple.	T	F
2.	The skin is a general word for a fruit.	T	F
3.	A pip is the small seed of a fruit.	T	F
4.	The peel is the outer covering of apples or pears.	T	F
5.	The husk is the dry, outer covering of grain.	T	F

6. The rind is the outer covering of certain fruit such as oranges and lemons.   T   F

7. Flesh is the soft, juicy substance of fruit.   T   F

8. The kernel is the most important part of an apple.   T   F

 EXERCISE 2

Complete the sentences with the correct answer.

1. The _____ is the part that can become a new plant.

   a. husk   b. peel   c. kernel

2. After taking the outer covers off the corn we were surrounded by a pile of _____.

   a. kernels   b. flesh   c. husks

3. Some watermelons have a million _____.

   a. pips   b. shells   c. rinds

4. Plums have hard _____.

   a. skin   b. flesh   c. stones

5. The _____ of the avocado is oily and rich.

   a. skin   b. flesh   c. kernel

6. Lemon _____ is often used in cakes.

   a. rind   b. husk   c. pip

7. The _____ of an egg is not good to eat.

   a. peel   b. husk   c. shell

8. A brown _____ often shows that a piece of fruit is old.

   a. skin   b. pit   c. kernel

9. A banana _____ is usually yellow when ripe.

   a. flesh   b. kernel   c. peel

Test on Living Things

Directions: Choose the answer that could best replace the underlined word or phrase without changing the meaning of the sentence.

1. A coconut palm's <u>blossom</u> is the main ingredient in several soft and alcoholic drinks.
    - (A) root
    - (B) flower
    - (C) fruit
    - (D) flesh

2. European cave <u>dwellers</u> depicted herds of mammoths with humps on their backs.
    - (A) inhabitants
    - (B) immigrants
    - (C) foes
    - (D) skins

3. Young nettle <u>shoots</u> have been used as food for a long time.
    - (A) seeds
    - (B) roots
    - (C) leaves
    - (D) kernels

4. A corn <u>kernel</u> should have at least 14 percent water so that it can pop under heat.
    - (A) husk
    - (B) seed
    - (C) rind
    - (D) bloom

5. By 1830, the lure of land had drawn increasing numbers of <u>pioneers</u> westward.
    - (A) dwellers
    - (B) competitors
    - (C) settlers
    - (D) allies

6. There was an old superstition that a sage plant will <u>droop</u> if its owner is unwell.
    - (A) peel off
    - (B) shoot up
    - (C) hang down
    - (D) dry up

7. The breadfruit is a round fruit with a rough <u>rind</u>, and a soft pulpy inside.
    - (A) skin
    - (B) husk
    - (C) shell
    - (D) bloom

8. Frederick W. Taylor was the <u>pioneer</u> of scientific management.
    - (A) immigrant
    - (B) inventor
    - (C) foe
    - (D) ally

9. After the first year at Plymouth in 1620–21, half the <u>colonists</u> died.
    - (A) companions
    - (B) enemies
    - (C) settlers
    - (D) foes

10. The almond, <u>native</u> to the Mediterranean, grows abundantly in California.
    - (A) relative
    - (B) pioneer
    - (C) original
    - (D) immigrant

11. When picking tea leaves, the <u>bud</u> and the two or three leaves below it are removed.
    - (A) old seedling
    - (B) husk
    - (C) rind
    - (D) new leaf

12. The cocoa trees bear football-shaped fruits with a <u>husk</u>.
    - (A) skin
    - (B) kernel
    - (C) seed
    - (D) shoot

CHAPTER 3

Theme Grouping: Time and Space

Reading Practice

Read the following passage.

In the United States, the Great Plains region has frequently been subject to periodic drought. As long as the plains were covered with short grass, the dry spells did little damage. But in 1889, the number of settlers in Oklahoma increased from a few thousand to 60,000, and more and more acres of protective grass were plowed to make room for crops. This took place during a period of abundant rainfall, and by 1900, the rich fertile soils of Oklahoma supported 390,000 people. Then in 1924 there was a prolonged drought. Vast stretches of grassland and crops lay scorched and the parched topsoil of Oklahoma was blown away by the wind. The skies darkened as clouds of dust, thousands of feet across, arose from the baked land. Formerly fertile soil was blown away as far as the Atlantic Ocean. The Great Plains had turned into dust. Henceforth, the area was given the name the

Dust Bowl. Over a million people with nothing left of their homes and farms migrated from Oklahoma and Arkansas to the West Coast.

 EXERCISE 1

Work with a partner, with a group, or alone to answer the following questions.

1. How often has the Great Plains region been subject to periodic drought?

Task

How often do you get droughts in your country?

2. What happened to the grassland and crops in the prolonged drought of 1924?

Task

What other things can be "scorched"?

3. What was the topsoil like during the drought of 1924?

Task

What is the difference between the words "parched" and "baked"?

4. What was the soil like before it was blown away?

Task

Give another word which is similar in meaning to "formerly."

5. What name was given to the area after the disaster?

Task

Which word in the passage tells us "from that time on"? Find three adjectives in the passages that are related to "heat and dryness."

Conversation Practice

Read the following conversation.

Norman:	Is it true that you're going on a camera safari in East Africa?
Julie:	Yes, it is. I travel to Africa **frequently.**
Norman:	I didn't know that. Do your trips require a lot of preparation **prior to** departure?
Julie:	Oh yes, but it's well worth it.
Norman:	Where will you be staying?
Julie:	I'll stay a few days in Nairobi, then I'll set off for the Northern Frontier District. **Eventually,** I'll make my way to Southwestern Kenya and Mount Kilimanjaro.
Norman:	It sounds exciting. What will the weather be like?
Julie:	For the most part it should be **balmy,** as I'm going at the end of the rainy season. However, conditions will often depend upon where I am at the time.
Norman:	You mean it'll be different from one place to another?
Julie:	Oh, yes. For example, the savannas, or plains, will be **arid** and the heat absolutely **scorching** on some days, while on Kilimanjaro it will be quite **chilly. Meanwhile** on the coast at Malindi the weather will be **sultry** and the air **humid.**

Norman:	Tell me about the animals.
Julie:	They're magnificent. In the Rift Valley, as far as the eye can see, the land is flat, the grass **parched**, and there are immense herds of animals—zebras, giraffes, and gazelles. At night, one can hear the hyenas and the **occasional** roar of a lion.
Norman:	It sounds wonderful and I hope I get to go to Africa someday!
Julie:	Well, if you really want to, then **eventually** you will. I'm sure of it.

 EXERCISE 2

Work with a partner, with a group, or alone to answer the following questions.

1. How often does Julie travel to Africa?

Task

What is the opposite of "frequently"? What other adverbs of time do you know?

2. When does she prepare for her trips?

Task

What does "prior to" mean? What is the opposite of "prior to"?

3. What is her final destination?

Task

What does "eventually" mean?

4. What will the weather be like for the most part?

Task

Give examples of two places and the times when the weather is "balmy."

5. What will the savannas, or plains, be like?

Task

Give two examples of areas in the world that are "arid."

6. What will the heat be like on the plains?

Task

Give examples of two places and the times when the heat is "scorching."

7. What will the weather be like on Kilimanjaro?

Task

Name two places and the times when the weather is "chilly."

8. What is the weather like on the coast of Malindi?

Task

Name two places in the world with this kind of weather.

9. What is the grass like in the flat Rift Valley?

Task

Give an example of something that is "parched."

A.   Adverbs of Time

sometimes	formerly	eventually
occasionally	previously	henceforth
frequently	prior to	simultaneously
		meanwhile

1. **sometimes** = not always, now and then.

     Ex.   We sometimes go to the movies on weekends.

2. **occasionally** = from time to time but not regularly or frequently.

     Ex.   I occasionally see a famous face at the opera.

3. **frequently** = repeated many times, especially at short intervals.

     Ex.   I must be getting old; I frequently forget where I am.

4. **formerly** = in earlier times.

     Ex.   The museum was formerly the house of the mayor.

5. **previously** = coming before (in time or order).

     Ex.   Had you previously taken the test before you came to the United States?

6. **prior to** = (formal adv. phrase) before.

     Ex.   No information was available prior to that date.

7. **eventually** = at last, ultimately, after a long time.

     Ex.   He eventually passed his drivers test after taking it eight times.

8. **henceforth** = from this time forward.

     Ex.   The committee has decided that henceforth a special test will have to be taken by new students.

9. **simultaneously** = happening at the same time.

     Ex.   The two events that were of interest to me were being shown simultaneously on television.

10. **meanwhile** = at the same time.

     Ex.   Some people are dying of hunger; meanwhile, others are throwing away food they don't eat.

EXERCISE 1

Circle T if the sentence is TRUE and F if the sentence is FALSE.

1.	Formerly means at an earlier date.	T	F
2.	Sometimes means not during the winter.	T	F
3.	Henceforth means from this time onwards.	T	F
4.	Frequently means often at short intervals.	T	F
5.	Eventually means late in the evening.	T	F
6.	Prior to means before in time.	T	F
7.	Meanwhile means at more or less the same time.	T	F
8.	Previously means coming after in time or order.	T	F

 **EXERCISE 2**

Complete the sentences with the correct answer.

1. It is winter in the north; _____, it is summer in the south.

   a. formerly   b. meanwhile   c. frequently

2. Mrs. Smith was _____ Miss Jones.

   a. meanwhile   b. formerly   c. sometimes

3. _____ eating that shrimp I felt fine.

   a. Prior to   b. Henceforth   c. Meanwhile

4. _____ he was an executive but now he works in a gas station.

   a. Previously   b. Sometimes   c. Frequently

5. We see each other _____ but not often.

   a. eventually   b. formerly   c. sometimes

6. The town of Blob has changed its name and will _____ be known as Blib.

   a. frequently   b. henceforth   c. eventually

7. I no longer go running as _____ as I used to.

   a. eventually   b. frequently   c. formerly

8. After looking for an hour she _____ found her purse.

   a. henceforth   b. sometimes   c. eventually

9. I _____ eat fish but more often I eat chicken.

   a. simultaneously   b. meanwhile   c. occasionally

10. The two runners crossed the line _____.

   a. sometimes   b. simultaneously   c. frequently

B. Dry and Not Dry

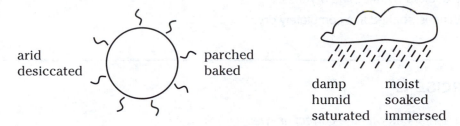

arid
desiccated

parched
baked

damp   moist
humid   soaked
saturated   immersed

1. **arid** = having little or no moisture, usually used for areas of land.

    Ex. Many areas of the southwestern United States are arid and desert-like.

2. **parched** = excessively dry and cracked through heat or drought.

    Ex. After five years with no rainfall, the farmland was parched.

3. **desiccated** = completely dry; without any moisture. It is usually said of animal and vegetable products that are dried and preserved.

    Ex. Sometimes using desiccated herbs when cooking is more convenient.

4. **baked** = when heat and dryness cause something to cook and become hard.

    Ex. The houses were built of baked mud bricks.

5. **damp** = not dry, but having a slight amount of moisture.

    Ex. Fabrics like linen are usually ironed while damp.

6. **moist** = a little wet; it is often used for food.

    Ex. The roast turkey was tasty and moist.

7. **humid** = having moisture, usually in warm air; it is often unpleasant.

    Ex. Humid air may be good for plants but is very disagreeable for humans.

8. **saturated** = completely wet or filled to the point it cannot take any more.

    Ex. His clothes were completely saturated with rain.

9. **soaked** = left in a liquid so that the moisture is absorbed.

    Ex. Soak the beans in water before you cook them.

10. **immersed** = completely covered in liquid or to be completely occupied in something.

    Ex. He was immersed in his work and did not even see me.

 EXERCISE 1

Circle T if the sentence is TRUE and F if the sentence is FALSE.

1. Animal and vegetable products dried out to be preserved are desiccated.	T	F
2. If something cracks for lack of water it is parched.	T	F
3. When the air is humid, it is very dry.	T	F
4. A little bit wet is damp.	T	F
5. To be immersed is to be totally covered by liquid.	T	F

6. Moist is wet enough that the liquid can be seen.   T   F
7. Baked is cooked by heat and dryness.   T   F
8. If something is soaked it is completely dry.   T   F

 EXERCISE 2

Complete the sentences with the correct answer.

1. After three days with no water his lips were _____.

   a. humid   b. parched   c. saturated

2. Camels store fat in their humps to travel in _____ lands.

   a. arid   b. soaked   c. baked

3. Before the thunderstorm, the air was very _____.

   a. humid   b. soaked   c. desiccated

4. After twenty minutes in the dryer, my socks were still _____.

   a. arid   b. immersed   c. damp

5. She _____ the bottle to remove the label.

   a. baked   b. soaked   c. parched

6. After a week of new information, his brain was _____.

   a. saturated   b. immersed   c. moist

7. After two months of burning sun, the plants were completely _____.

   a. humid   b. arid   c. desiccated

8. They _____ the bread in a hot oven.

   a. immersed   b. baked   c. soaked

9. She was not crying but her eyes were _____.

   a. arid   b. moist   c. soaked

10. To wash sheep they are _____ in a special bath or dip.

   a. baked   b. immersed   c. parched

C. Hot and Not Hot

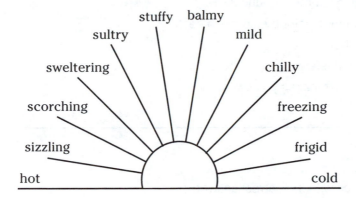

1. **scorching** = so hot that it burns the surface making it change its color.

    Ex. The scorching heat had turned the grass brown.

2. **sizzling** = extremely hot. Sizzling also refers to the sound of food frying over a fire.

    Ex. There seems to be a spell of sizzling weather every summer in the southern states.

3. **sweltering** = very hot and uncomfortable causing one to sweat.

    Ex. It is difficult to exercise in the sweltering heat of the jungle.

4. **sultry** = a hot and moist type of weather with no breeze.

    Ex. In the sultry days of August, everyone turns on a fan or air conditioning for relief.

5. **stuffy** = having air which is not fresh.

    Ex. Crowded with students and with no windows open, the classroom felt very stuffy.

6. **balmy** = a soft, pleasant, refreshing type of air often with aromatic smells from trees.

    Ex. We had breakfast in the garden on that balmy spring morning.

7. **mild** = neither too hot nor too cold.

    Ex. Winters are usually mild on the island because of the ocean current.

8. **chilly** = cold enough to make one shiver a little.

    Ex. The early mornings were quite chilly in the mountains.

9. **frigid** = intense cold with continuous low temperatures below 32°F.

    Ex. The North and South poles have a frigid climate.

10. **freezing** = very cold, icy weather.

    Ex. The freezing temperatures in spring damaged the orange trees.

 EXERCISE 1

Circle T if the sentence is TRUE and F if the sentence is FALSE.

1. Balmy means smelling like trees.   T   F
2. Wet and cold weather is sultry.   T   F

3. Something frigid is always frozen below 32°F.　　　　　　　T　F
4. Something freezing is down around 32°F.　　　　　　　　　T　F
5. Scorching is to change color by too much heat.　　　　　　T　F
6. Mild is extremely hot.　　　　　　　　　　　　　　　　T　F
7. Stuffy is hot and airless.　　　　　　　　　　　　　　　T　F
8. Sweltering is so hot it makes you sweat.　　　　　　　　　T　F

 EXERCISE 2

Complete the sentences with the correct answer.

1. It was _____ in the meat freezer.

   a. balmy　　　　　　　　b. frigid　　　　　　　　c. sizzling

2. Tropical countries generally have a _____ climate.

   a. sultry　　　　　　　　b. freezing　　　　　　　c. mild

3. It was too cold for my car to start in the _____ weather.

   a. freezing　　　　　　　b. scorching　　　　　　c. chilly

4. The food was so hot it was still _____ when it reached us.

   a. sizzling　　　　　　　b. chilly　　　　　　　　c. sweltering

5. The temperature was _____, neither too hot nor too cold.

   a. balmy　　　　　　　　b. stuffy　　　　　　　　c. mild

6. With no air conditioning it was _____ in my car.

   a. mild　　　　　　　　　b. sweltering　　　　　　c. frigid

7. The _____ heat from the fire ruined my boots.

   a. chilly　　　　　　　　b. balmy　　　　　　　　c. scorching

8. In the evening it can be _____ enough for a jacket.

   a. freezing　　　　　　　b. chilly　　　　　　　　c. balmy

9. After a hot day, the evening cooled to a _____ temperature.

   a. balmy　　　　　　　　b. stuffy　　　　　　　　c. sweltering

10. With twenty people in the small room, the air was _____.

   a. mild　　　　　　　　　b. stuffy　　　　　　　　c. sultry

48

Test on Time and Space

Choose the answer that could best replace the underlined word or phrase without changing the meaning of the sentence.

1. Chloroform was <u>simultaneously</u> invented by the American Samuel Guthrie and the German Justus Liebig in 1830.

   (A) now and then   (B) in earlier times

   (C) at the same time   (D) little by little

2. In 1864 George Pullman designed a sleeping car that <u>eventually</u> saw widespread use.

   (A) previously   (B) ultimately

   (C) familiarly   (D) simultaneously

3. Freshwater turtles can survive in <u>frigid</u> waters for three months without oxygen.

   (A) balmy   (B) sultry

   (C) freezing   (D) sweltering

4. <u>Prior to</u> World War I, 20 percent of American homes had electricity.

   (A) Before   (B) During

   (C) After   (D) Despite

5. The flowering pebble is a plant that looks like a stone and grows in <u>arid</u> areas.

   (A) saturated   (B) damp

   (C) dry   (D) immersed

6. The <u>parched</u> landscape of salt flats is often used to break world land speed records.

   (A) dried   (B) soaked

   (C) sultry   (D) chilly

7. <u>Previously</u>, the economy of the United States was agrarian.

   (A) Formerly   (B) Occasionally

   (C) Eventually   (D) Frequently

8. Coconuts are often used in <u>desiccated</u> form in baking.

   (A) chilly   (B) freezing

   (C) dried   (D) baked

9. The breadfruit does well in hot and <u>humid</u> climates.

   (A) arid   (B) damp

   (C) soaked   (D) desiccated

10. <u>Formerly</u> a palace, the Louvre was made a museum after the French Revolution.

    (A) Henceforth   (B) Eventually

    (C) Previously   (D) Frequently

11. The water table has a level called the zone of <u>saturation</u>.

    (A) freezing   (B) humidity

    (C) soaking   (D) dryness

CHAPTER 4

Everyday and Specific Vocabulary

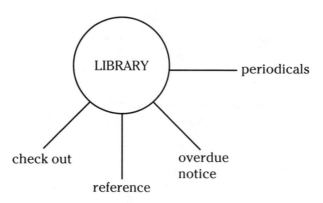

Learning vocabulary in sets of words that are related to each other under one area makes it easier for you to learn words. It makes your study more structured than learning words in a random way. It also gives you a clue to the meaning of an unknown word. For example, when you see the term "check out" under the subject "library," you will realize it is something you do when you are in a library.

Learning the sets of words in this section will help you with the short dialogues in the Listening Comprehension section of the TOEFL®.

Conversation Practice

Read the following conversation.

Lisa: My goodness, Carol, what are you doing at the library so late?
Carol: I'm doing research for my term paper.
Lisa: What course is it for?
Carol: Introduction to Psychology.
Lisa: Who's your professor?
Carol: Dr. Kent is teaching the course.
Lisa: I know her. I attended one of her seminars last month.
Carol: Really? Was it offered here on campus?
Lisa: Yes, it was held in the auditorium.
Carol: Did you like it?
Lisa: Oh, very much. As a matter of fact, I thought her lectures were so interesting that I've registered for one of her classes next semester.
Carol: That's terrific. I think she's a good instructor, too.
Lisa: I'd better let you get back to work now. When is your assignment due?
Carol: It's due tomorrow afternoon and I've still got two more resources to find before the library closes.
Lisa: I wish I could help you, but I have to get back to the dorm and start studying for my history final.
Carol: Thanks, but I'll be all right. Good luck on your test.
Lisa: Thanks. Good luck on your paper. I'll see you during semester break.

 EXERCISE 1

Work with a partner, with a group, or alone to answer the following questions. Be prepared to explain your answers.

1. Where is this conversation taking place?

2. What is Carol doing?

3. How does Lisa know Dr. Kent?

4. Where was the seminar?

5. What has Lisa done for next semester?

6. What does Carol think about Dr. Kent?

7. What does Carol still have to do before the library closes?

8. Why does Lisa have to get back to the dorm?

9. When will Lisa and Carol see each other?

Task

Read the conversation again. Write down or underline 15 words related to COLLEGE/UNIVERSITY. From these words:

- Write down two words that are places.
- Give another word for an instructor.
- Find another word that is a test.

Reading Practice

Read the following advertisement.

Our health care program provides complete medical care and quality you can count on. Your hospital coverage includes nursing and physicians' care, surgery, therapy, laboratory tests, and medicines. We want to keep you well by preventing illness, so your benefits include regular checkups, and vision and hearing examinations. You're covered for emergencies in your hometown and when you travel anywhere in the world. You can count on our program to give you the health care you want and need in our many medical facilities nationwide. Most of our more than 90 medical offices provide routine care, as well as lab, pharmacy, and X-ray services. Our well-trained medical staff and specialists will give you the best treatment available.

 EXERCISE 2

Work with a partner, a group, or alone to answer the following questions.

1. What does the health program provide?
2. Write six things that the hospital coverage includes.
3. What three benefits are included for preventing illness?
4. What four things do most of their more than 90 medical facilities provide?
5. Who will give you the best treatment available?

Task

Read the advertisement again. List 20 words related to HEALTH CARE.

STRATEGIES

- Making lists of words related to one subject will help you remember them. Keep adding to your list as soon as you learn another word related to that area.

- Use a technique that will help you remember the words. You may memorize them, or use visual or other clues to help you remember.

- Words related to people and places are tested in the short dialogues and also appear in the longer conversations in the Listening Comprehension of the TOEFL® section.

In the short dialogues listen for a word that will be a clue to either the person's occupation or the location.

EXAMPLE

Man: Is there a cafeteria on campus?

Woman: Sure. It's over there next to the bookstore.

Question: Where does this conversation take place?

(A) A hospital.   (B) A university.

(C) A hotel.   (D) A street.

The word "campus" here is the clue that it is a university. The other words "cafeteria" and "bookstore" can be found anywhere.

In the longer conversations, too, word clues will help you connect the conversation to a speaker or a location.

Everyday and Specific Vocabulary

It is important to know as many words as possible connected with a profession, a location, or a subject area. In the Listening Comprehension section of the test, the short dialogues may be followed by questions about:

a. location: Where does this conversation take place?
b. occupation: What's the man's/woman's occupation?

EXAMPLE

You hear:

> Paul: Where can I register?
> Lin: Over there, next to where it says "tuition fees."

Question: Where does this conversation probably take place?

You read:

(A) On a college campus.   (B) In a museum.

(C) At the hospital.   (D) At a hotel.

The answer is "A." Although people can register in a hotel or at a hospital, nothing indicates this conversation takes place in a hotel. The combination of "tuition" and "register" indicates "A" is correct.

Identifying Locations

Some key words will help you identify where the conversation takes place.

EXAMPLE

Hotel

suite	reservation	room service
wake-up call	check out	lobby
reception desk	to page	doorkeeper
to book	porter	

Doctor's Clinic

waiting room	consulting room	checkup	vaccine
shot	dressing	bandage	patient
physician	treatment	diagnosis	convalescent

 EXERCISE 1

Under each of the locations below choose three words from the following box. Some words in the box may not be related to the location.

A. *Bank*

1. _____

2. _____

3. _____

B. *Restaurant*

1. _____

2. _____

3. _____

withdrawal	house special	voltage	balance
dressing	deposit slip	tip	sublet

Now add three more words of your own to each list.

C. *Garage*

1. _____

2. _____

3. _____

D. *School*

1. _____

2. _____

3. _____

tune-up	tuition	schedule of classes
brake fluid	registration	radiator
contract	fare	prescription

Now add three more words of your own to each list.

E. *Supermarket*

1. _____

2. _____

3. _____

F. *Clothing Store*

1. _____

2. _____

3. _____

aisle salesperson	charge account exchange	deli drill	produce citation

Now add three more words of your own to each list.

G. Theater

1. _____

2. _____

3. _____

H. Post Office

1. _____

2. _____

3. _____

special delivery box office	registered money order	row round trip	usher pump

Now add three more words of your own to each list.

I. Courtroom

1. _____

2. _____

3. _____

J. Library

1. _____

2. _____

3. _____

jury prosecutor	reference nonfiction	periodicals gates	case departures

Now add three more words of your own to each list.

K. On a Bus

1. _____

2. _____

3. _____

L. Zoo

1. _____

2. _____

3. _____

schedule duty-free	fare feeding time	transfer tenants	aviary cages

Now add three more words of your own to each list.

Identifying Occupations

Some key words can help you identify the occupation of a person.

EXAMPLE

Teacher

midterm	finals	grades
research paper	assignment	instructor
lecture	seminar	course

 EXERCISE 2

Match the occupations in the box with the words associated with them.

police officer	college student
nurse	car salesperson
electrician	travel agent
plumber	apartment manager
dentist	gas station attendant

A. _____

1. fill it up

2. unleaded

3. pump

B. _____

1. cavity

2. extraction

3. filling

C. _____

1. faucet

2. pipe

3. clog

D. _____

1. utilities

2. deposit

3. refundable

E. _____

1. speeding ticket

2. illegal turn

3. driver's license

F. _____

1. thermometer

2. blood pressure

3. vaccine

G. _____

1. good mileage

2. new model

3. monthly payment

H. _____

1. brochure

2. round trip

3. cruise

I. _____   J. _____
   1. freshman   1. fuse
   2. graduate   2. wire
   3. tuition   3. socket

Test on Everyday and Specific Vocabulary

Choose the correct answer.

1. Man: What seems to be the problem, ma'am?

   Woman: This sink is clogged up and the faucet is dripping.

   Question: What kind of work does the man probably do?

   (A) He's an engineer.   (B) He's a mechanic.
   (C) He's a plumber   (D) He's an electrician.

2. Woman: Where can I find the course books for Spanish 101?

   Man: They're in aisle 3, under languages.

   Question: Where is this conversation taking place?

   (A) In a library.   (B) In a bookstore.

   (C) At a travel agency.   (D) In a supermarket.

3. Woman: Could you fill it up with unleaded?

   Man: Sure. Do you want me to check under the hood?

   Question: What kind of work does the man do?

   (A) He's a plumber.   (B) He's a dentist.
   (C) He's a gas station attendant.   (D) He's an engineer.

4. Man: I'm looking for the dressings.

   Woman: They're in aisle 5 next to the produce.

   Question: Where does this conversation take place?

   (A) In a hospital.   (B) In a clothing store.
   (C) In a restaurant.   (D) In a supermarket.

5. Woman: I'd like to exchange these two items.

   Man: Do you have the receipts for them?

   Question: Where is this conversation probably taking place?

   (A) At a library.   (B) At a department store.
   (C) At a bank.   (D) In a theater.

6. Woman: Have you had an appointment with us before?

   Man: Yes, I came in for a flu shot last year.

   Question: What is the woman's occupation?

   (A) She's a nurse.   (B) She's a teller.

   (C) She's a dentist.   (D) She's a hair stylist.

7. Man: Will there be any breaks during this play?

   Woman: Yes, there will be a short intermission after each act.

   Question: Where is this conversation taking place?

   (A) In a theater.   (B) In a supermarket.

   (C) In a library.   (D) In a park.

8. Woman: Could you have fresh towels brought to my room, please?

   Man: Yes ma'am. I'll send someone right away.

   Question: Where is this conversation taking place?

   (A) In a department store.   (B) At a restaurant.

   (C) At a school.   (D) In a hotel.

9. Man: I'd like a book of stamps, please.

   Woman: Here you are. That will be $5.80.

   Question: Where is this conversation taking place?

   (A) At a drugstore   (B) At an art gallery.

   (C) At a post office.   (D) At the cinema.

10. Man: Have you decided what you'd like?

    Woman: Yes, I'd like a cup of tea and a slice of peach pie.

    Question: What is the man's occupation?

    (A) He's a truck driver.   (B) He's a store clerk.

    (C) He's a waiter.   (D) He's a baker.

11. Woman: The water looks great today.

    Man: I can't wait to jump on my surfboard.

    Question: Where is this conversation taking place?

    (A) On a busy street.   (B) At the beach.

    (C) At an amusement park.   (D) At a concert.

12. Man: I'd like to add one more city to my tour of Europe.

    Woman: I've already made your reservations, but let me see what I can do for you.

    Question: What kind of work does the woman do?

    (A) She's a teacher.   (B) She's a travel agent.

    (C) She's an architect.   (D) She's a writer.

13. Man: Did I miss anything while I was buying the hot dogs and sodas?

    Woman: Yes, our team scored a touchdown!

    Question: Where is this conversation taking place?

    (A) At a shopping center.   (B) At the circus.

    (C) At a cafe.   (D) At a stadium.

14. Woman: The X-rays show you have no cavities.

    Man: Thank goodness. I hate to have my teeth drilled.

    Question: What is the woman's occupation?

    (A) She's a dentist.   (B) She's a carpenter.

    (C) She's an engineer.   (D) She's a computer operator.

15. Man: Are you enjoying this modern art exhibit?

    Woman: Not really. I prefer the Impressionist painters.

    Question: Where is this conversation taking place?

    (A) On a bus.   (B) At a hair salon.

    (C) In a bookstore.   (D) At a museum.

CHAPTER **5**

Roots

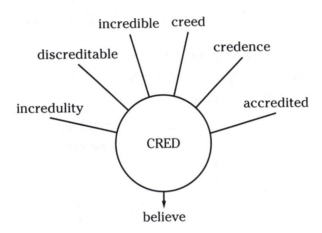

The root of a word contains the basic meaning. Prefixes and suffixes can be added to a root. For example, the root *cred* means "believe," so the English word "credible" means "believable." Learning the roots of words will help you work out the meaning of words you do not know and will consequently help you with *all* parts of the TOEFL® test.

Since there are a great number of roots from which words stem in English, the most common ones are given for you to work with in this section. We will start by looking at four of these roots (*cred, spec, duc, ced*) and work with some of the words they create.

Reading Practice

Read the following passage.

Some theories of laughter emphasize its ability to reduce tension and emotion. You have probably been in a tense group situation when someone suddenly made exactly the right joke to defuse the mood and make everyone laugh. Laughter seems to produce some beneficial biological responses, possibly stimulating the immune system or starting the flow of endorphins, the pain-killing chemicals in the brain.

Other theories emphasize the cognitive components of humor. When you laugh at a problem, you are putting it in a new perspective—seeing its silly aspects—and gaining control over it.

Having a sense of humor, however, is not the same as smiling all the time or "putting on a happy face." Many women, in particular, feel they have to smile, smile, smile, to put others at ease, but often this social smile masks feelings of insecurity and unhappiness. For humor to be effective in coping with stress, a person must actually use it in a stressful situation—seeing or inventing funny aspects of serious events and having the ability to laugh at them.

 EXERCISE 1

Work with a partner, with a group, or alone to answer these questions.

1. What ability of laughter do some theories emphasize?

Task

The word root *duct* means "to lead." What is the connection in meaning between *duct* and "reduce"?

2. What kind of biological response does laughter produce?

Task

Do you think *bene* means "good" or "bad"? Find two other words which begin with *bene-*. What do these words mean?

3. When you laugh at a problem, what are you doing?

Task

What letters do the words "perspective" and "aspect" have in common? Find two other words with these letters in them. What is the connection in their meaning?

 EXERCISE 2

Work with a partner, with a group, or alone. Read the following sentences and underline the following roots:

cred	spec	dic	vis/vid

1. In 1815 Napoleon was defeated and was forced to abdicate.

2. Panama was chosen as the most likely prospect for a canal linking the Caribbean and the Pacific because of its location.

3. Presbyterianism is a Protestant sect, based on Calvinist creed, which states that salvation is predetermined.

4. Ernest Hemingway's unemotional and cynical style is evident in his novels *The Sun Also Rises* and *For Whom the Bell Tolls*.

These roots have the following meanings:

cred = to believe
spec = to look
dic = to say or speak
vis/vid = to see

Discuss how these roots are connected to the meanings of the words above. You may use a dictionary.

STRATEGIES

- Most word roots are never used alone. They may have prefixes and suffixes attached to them.

EXAMPLE

> The root *dict* meaning "to say or speak" is not used alone. Prefixes like *pre, contra* (predict, contradict) or suffixes like *-ation, –ator* (dictation, dictator) are added to it.

- At first you may not see how a particular word grew from the word root. But when you begin to analyze the word, you will see the connection.

EXAMPLE

> The word "revolve" comes from the root "volv" meaning "turn" or "roll." It is easy to see the connection between "revolve" and its root volv. The word "devolve" means "to pass on to another person," and has the idea of "roll." The word "evolution" means "how something changes over time" and has the idea of turning into something else. The idea of "turning" or "rolling" will change in each word, but the connection is the same.

- Once you recognize word roots, you will see connections among many words. This will make it easier for you to understand and remember their meanings.

- Study the word roots in this chapter and the words they produce over a period of weeks. Try to learn a number of word roots each day. Review the roots you have learned before and try to use them in speech or writing.

- Every time you look up a word in the dictionary, look at its word root (most roots in English come from Latin or Greek). Add new roots to the roots given in this section.

A. Root: *Cred*

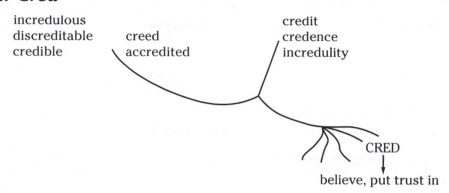

incredulous
discreditable
credible

creed
accredited

credit
credence
incredulity

CRED

believe, put trust in

1. **incredulous** = showing disbelief.

    Ex.   The people listening to his strange story were incredulous.

2. **discreditable** = disgraceful or shameful behavior.

    Ex.   Because of the banker's discreditable behavior, a lot of customers changed to another bank.

3. **creed** = a set of beliefs or principles, usually religious.

    Ex.   People of all creeds gathered in union to help the cause.

4. **accredited** = certified as being of a certain good standard.

    Ex.   He went to an accredited high school.

5. **credible** = believable, trustworthy.

    Ex.   A credible explanation was given for the changes made.

6. **credit** = belief, trust, honor and recognition given to effort or work.

    Ex.   With her outstanding grades in her studies and outstanding ability in sports, she was a credit to her school.

7. **credence** = belief; acceptance as being true.

    Ex.   The rumor got widespread credence throughout the country.

8. **incredulity** = the act of not believing.

    Ex.   He looked at me with incredulity in his eyes when I told him he had won the lottery.

 EXERCISE 1

Complete the definition with the correct answer.

1. Something which can be believed is _____.

    a.   accredited   b.   credible

2. Something discreditable cannot be _____.

    a.   believed   b.   shameful

3. To tell the truth and work hard does you _____.

    a.   credence   b.   credit

4. To have a creed is to have a _____.
   a. set of beliefs　　　　　　　　　　b. good standards

5. Incredulity is a _____.
   a. lack of trust　　　　　　　　　　b. lack of belief

6. An accredited school _____.
   a. is certified　　　　　　　　　　b. borrows money

7. _____ is being accepted as true.
   a. Credit　　　　　　　　　　　　b. Credence

 EXERCISE 2

Choose the correct word to complete each sentence.

1. If you want your car fixed properly, go to an (accredited / incredulous) mechanic.
2. I can understand your (incredulity / credit) but you are the new king!
3. Such (credible / discreditable) behavior can only ruin our company.
4. The school children gained great (incredulity / credit) by helping the old folks.
5. Sitting in her palace, listening to her story of hardship and poverty, the visitors were (incredulous / discreditable).
6. You never know what he is thinking because he follows no special (creed / credit).
7. He may look like he is telling the truth, but we have no reason to give (incredulity / credence) to his story.
8. We should win in court because our witnesses are more (accredited / credible) than theirs.

B.　Roots: *Spect, Spec*

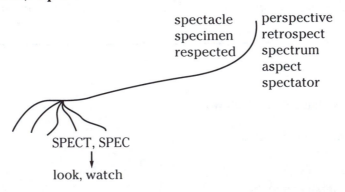

1. **perspective** = a way in which something is looked at or judged.

   Ex. A tribesman in Africa looks at time from a different perspective than an American businessman.

2. **retrospect** = a look back at the past.

> *Ex.* As we take on responsibilities in life, our teenage years in retrospect seem carefree.

3. **spectrum** = a range of colors in the order of their wavelengths.

> *Ex.* Ultra-violet rays are beyond the range of the visible spectrum.

4. **aspect** = a look at something from one side.

> *Ex.* There is a television series on the different aspects of life in the United States.

5. **spectacle** = a scene or show which attracts the eye by its size, color.

> *Ex.* The Independence Day firework show was quite a spectacle.

6. **specimen** = a sample; a single typical thing to be shown or tested.

> *Ex.* The specimen of rock from the moon went through multiple tests.

7. **respected** = worthy to be looked up to and admired.

> *Ex.* The teacher was highly respected by his students.

8. **spectator** = a person who watches an event or a sport.

> *Ex.* The spectators cheered as the famous player appeared on the field.

 ## EXERCISE 1

Replace the underlined words with the words below.

spectrum	aspect	spectacle	specimen
spectators	perspective	a respected	retrospect

1. All the <u>people who were watching</u> cheered when our team scored a goal.
2. Having to earn money is just one <u>side</u> of modern life.
3. Whether you like or hate modern art depends on your <u>way of looking at it</u>.
4. In <u>looking back at the past</u>, we should have kept our 1952 Cadillac.
5. The mayor is <u>an admired</u> member of our community.
6. When you get sick the doctor will often send a <u>sample</u> of your blood for analysis.
7. The beautiful diamond flashed all colors of the <u>range of colors in the order of their wavelengths</u>.
8. As we reached the top of the hill, we gazed at the <u>amazing scene of size and color</u> of the armies lined up in the valley below.

 ## EXERCISE 2

The word with the "spec" root in each sentence is not correct. Cross out the word and write the correct word above it and make the necessary changes to the articles.

1. The spectrum attracts you with its size and color.
2. Respected is looking back at the past.

3. A range of colors in the order of their wavelengths is a specimen.
4. Retrospect is the way things are looked at or judged.
5. A specimen is one point of view.
6. An aspect is someone who watches a sports event.
7. A spectator is someone you look up to and admire.
8. A perspective is a sample of something.

C. Roots: *Duc, Duct*

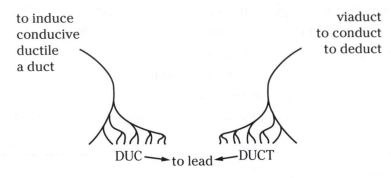

to induce
conducive
ductile
a duct

viaduct
to conduct
to deduct

DUC → to lead ← DUCT

1. **to conduct** = to lead.

    Ex. The inspector was conducted around the factory.

2. **conducive** = helpful; that contributes to.

    Ex. A dark room is more conducive to sleep than a bright one.

3. **a duct** = a tube or canal that carries fluids, or one that carries electric power, telephone cables, etc.

    Ex. Most glands in human bodies have ducts to carry their secretions.

4. **to deduct** = to subtract, or take away.

    Ex. Income tax is deducted from the paycheck of a wage earner.

5. **ductile** = easily lead; pliable.

    Ex. Copper is a ductile metal.

6. **to induce** = to cause an effect.

    Ex. Political repression and poverty induced many people to leave their homeland and emigrate.

7. **viaduct** = a long high bridge which carries a road or railroad.

    Ex. Some of the old viaducts are not high enough for today's tall trucks to go under.

8. **aqueduct** = a system of canals and bridges which carry water.

    Ex. Some of the aqueducts built by the Romans still bring water to modern cities.

EXERCISE 1

Match the words in Column A with their definitions in Column B.

Column A

_____ 1. a duct

_____ 2. ductile

_____ 3. induce

_____ 4. aqueduct

_____ 5. conduct

_____ 6. viaduct

_____ 7. conducive

_____ 8. deduct

Column B

a. a system of canals

b. helpful

c. to lead

d. a bridge that carries a road

e. to take away

f. a tube or canal

g. easily lead

h. to cause an effect

 EXERCISE 2

Complete the sentences with the correct answer.

1. No one knows what _____ the millionaire to give his money to strangers.

   a. conducted   b. induced

2. Our new puppy has a very _____ personality and will be easy to train.

   a. ductile   b. conducive

3. The waiter _____ the guests to their table.

   a. deducted   b. conducted

4. Fire regulations require electrical wires to be run inside a _____ when they are used outside the house.

   a. viaduct   b. duct

5. Los Angeles is built in a desert and water has to be brought to it by a huge _____.

   a. viaduct   b. aqueduct

6. Some policies are more _____ to peace than others.

   a. conducive   b. conducted

7. To cross the canyon they had to build a tall _____.

   a. aqueduct   b. viaduct

8. Every month the bank _____ a service charge from my account.

   a. deducts   b. conducts

D. Roots: *Ced, Cess*

procedure   secede
precedent   process
antecedent   concede
recede   successive

CED, CESS

to go, move along

1. **procedure** = a particular way or method of doing something.

    Ex. To take a class in this college you have to follow the registration procedure.

2. **precedent** = a past action or case that sets an example or rule for cases in the future.

    Ex. In his defense the lawyer referred to a similar case in 1952 that established a precedent in favor of his client.

3. **antecedent** = that which has gone on at an earlier time.

    Ex. The antecedents of Halloween go back to pagan festivals.

4. **successive** = (adj) following one after the other.

    Ex. She was absent from school for four successive days.

5. **to recede** = to move back or to shrink in size.

    Ex. When gums recede, it is wise to see the dentist.

6. **to secede** = to officially withdraw from a group, union, or organization that is usually political or religious.

    Ex. When a state in a nation secedes, civil war may break out.

7. **to process** = to treat in a particular organized way.

    Ex. Photographic film has to be processed before we get the pictures.

8. **to concede** = to give victory or possession to someone else.

    Ex. The challenger conceded victory to the president in the election race.

 EXERCISE **1**

Complete the definitions with the correct word.

procedure	precedent	antecedent	secede
concede	successive	recede	process

1. A/An _____ is something which has happened before.

2. A/An _____ is a past action which sets an example for the future.

3. To _____ is to move back.

4. Things that are _____ follow each other.

5. The loser has to _____ a contest to the winner.

6. It can take several weeks to _____ a new passport application.

7. A/An _____ is a particular system to do something.

8. To _____ is to withdraw from a political group.

EXERCISE 2

Choose the correct word to complete the sentence.

1. It will take six months to _____ your request for a permit.

   a. concede   b. process

2. Our team were champions for four _____ seasons.

   a. antecedent   b. successive

3. As far as we know, there is no _____ for a mouse killing a tiger.

   a. precedent   b. process

4. If too many states _____ from the republic it will break up.

   a. recede   b. secede

5. I have to _____ that you know more about astrophysics than I do.

   a. concede   b. recede

6. The _____ for repairing the engine was very complicated.

   a. precedent   b. procedure

EXERCISE 3

Work with a partner or a group. Find two examples of words for each of the roots below. Then check your examples in a dictionary.

Root	Area of Meaning	Examples
agr	land	
amb(u)l	walk	
anima	life, spirit	
anthro	man, mankind	
aster	star	
auto	self	
bene	well	
bibl	book	
bio	life	
brev	short	
capit	head	
carn	flesh	
ced, cess	go	

Root	Area of Meaning	Examples
cide	kill	
civ	citizen	
chrome	color	
chron	time	
corp	body	
cosm	world, order	
cred	believe	
cycl	wheel, circle	
demo	people	
dic, dict	say, speak	
domin	master	
duc, duct	lead	
dynam	power	
fac, fact	do, make	
flex	bend	
form	shape	
fort	strong	
gamy	marriage	
gen	birth	
geo	earth	
graph, gram	write	
hetero	other, different	
homo	same	
hydro	water	
leg	law	
loc	place	
log, logy	speech, study, word	
man, manu	hand	
mar	sea	
mater, matri	mother	
medi	middle	
mob	move	
nom	name	
omni	all	
pater, patri	father	
pathy	feeling	
phon	sound	
port	carry	
rupt	break	
scope	watch	
scrib, script	write	
spect	look, watch	
tax, tact	arrange, order	
temper	time	
term	end, limit	
theo	god	
tract	draw, pull	
urb	city	
vene, vent	come, go	
vid, vis	see	
voc, vok	call	
volu, volv	turn	

EXERCISE 4

Read the following passage and find the roots of the words in bold print.

Birds have two basic types of sounds—songs and calls. Songs are usually more complex than calls and are utilized **primarily** by adult males during breeding season to establish territories or **attract** mates. Calls are normally simple notes, single or repeated, **vocalized** by males and females in all seasons to express alarm or maintain contact with mates, offspring, or other birds of the same species. All songs and most calls are distinctive, and with concentrated study and practice, **ornithologists** learn to identify many birds by their sounds and call them as well.

1. What does "primarily" in the passage mean?

_____

2. What does the word "attract" mean?

_____

3. What does the word "vocalized" mean in the passage?

_____

4. What do you think an "ornithologist" studies?

_____

EXERCISE 5

Use roots and a dictionary to find the answers to these questions.

1. What does an anthropologist study?

_____

2. What do we call a person who studies handwriting?

_____

3. What do we call a person who studies the stars?

_____

4. What does "inductive" reasoning mean?

_____

5. What do we call events in order of "time"?

_____

Test on Roots

Choose the answer that could best replace the underlined word or phrase without changing the meaning of the sentence.

1. Violet and red are at the opposite ends of the spectrum.
   - (A) range of sounds
   - (B) types of taste
   - (C) range of colors
   - (D) boundary of light

2. Sedatives calm a person without actually inducing sleep.
   - (A) prolonging
   - (B) subsiding
   - (C) getting
   - (D) causing

3. The removal of cataracts in the eyes by laser has become a common procedure.
   - (A) belief
   - (B) method
   - (C) improvement
   - (D) regulation

4. Soya beans are being processed to look and taste like meat.
   - (A) immersed
   - (B) dehydrated
   - (C) colored
   - (D) treated

5. F. D. Roosevelt was the only man to have been elected president of the United States four successive times.
   - (A) significant
   - (B) consecutive
   - (C) notable
   - (D) symmetrical

6. Specimens of bone are used for DNA typing.
   - (A) samples
   - (B) spots
   - (C) units
   - (D) discoloration

7. In 1861 seven states seceded from the Union and formed the Confederate States of America.
   - (A) developed
   - (B) emerged
   - (C) succeeded
   - (D) withdrew

8. Thousands of prospectors came to the newly formed territory of California after gold was discovered at Sutter's Mill in 1848.
   - (A) people looking for gold
   - (B) people who were experts
   - (C) people who wanted land
   - (D) people with no hope

9. Aqueducts built during the Roman Empire may still be seen in many parts of Europe.
   - (A) baths
   - (B) water canals
   - (C) roads
   - (D) air pipes

10. The Capitol, built on a hill in Washington, D.C., is the seat of the U.S. legislature.
    - (A) military power
    - (B) men of education
    - (C) lawmakers
    - (D) business people

11. In the United States, a party can nominate a single candidate for office.
    - (A) refuse
    - (B) keep
    - (C) change
    - (D) name

12. Guam, an island in the West Pacific, was ceded to the United States.
    - (A) given over to
    - (B) attacked by
    - (C) ruled by
    - (D) influenced by

CHAPTER 6

Theme Grouping: Thought and Communication

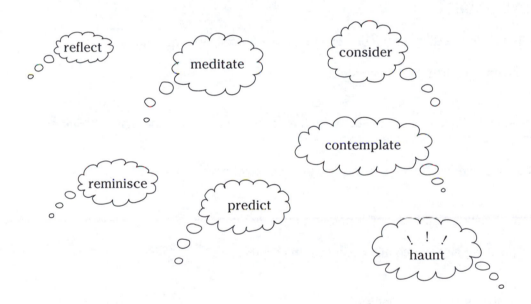

Another way of building your vocabulary is by looking at words with similar meanings in themes. For example, if we take the theme "Thinking and Remembering," we find there are several words that mean "to think" but each is slightly different in its meaning and use. The verb "to reflect" means "to think" and is used when thinking over something carefully, whereas the verb "to meditate" is used when thinking deeply about one matter and is often used in religion.

In this section there are different themes with exercises that accompany them. Since only a certain number of themes can be covered in this book, it is suggested that you start to make your own themes with the use of a dictionary in order to continue to build your vocabulary.

Reading Practice

Read the following passage.

The coyote used to live in the western part of the United States. Despite its persecution by farmers who have assumed that the coyote has been responsible for the killing of their livestock, the coyote has survived. Today the coyote is widespread from Alaska to New York, and in towns as well as in the wild.

Scientifically, the coyote is *Canis latrans,* barking dog, so-called because apart from the domestic dog it is the only member of the dog family that habitually barks. Foxes, wolves, and jackals only bark at specific times. The renowned call of the coyote at night is a familiar scene in a Western movie. In the evening coyotes sing in chorus. One starts with a series of short barks, gradually increasing in volume until they merge into a yell. Other coyotes join in and the chorus continues for a minute or two. After a pause, the chorus starts again. Two or three coyotes may meet each night to sing and the haunting effect of the songs of several such groups over the countryside is unique.

 EXERCISE 1

Work with a partner, with a group, or alone to answer the following questions.

1. Where can you find the coyote today?

Task

What do you think is the difference between the words "widespread" and "usual"? Find another word in the passage that is similar in meaning to "usual."

2. What kind of effect do the songs of several groups of coyotes have?

Task

What kinds of things would "haunt" a person's memory?

3. Can anything else create this effect over the countryside?

Task

Name three things that are "unique."

Conversation Practice

Read the following conversation.

Scott: You look serious today, Regina. Is something wrong?
Regina: Oh, no. I was just sitting here **reflecting** on life.
Scott: **Contemplating** your future?
Regina: How did you know?
Scott: It's a **familiar** thought to me. After all, we'll be starting college in a few weeks, and we'll have to make some **crucial** decisions.

Regina:	Have you decided on your major?
Scott:	No. I've **speculated** on several careers, but I haven't decided on one yet. And you? Do you have any ideas what you want to do?
Regina:	To a certain extent, yes. I've made certain **fundamental** decisions.
Scott:	Such as?
Regina:	Well, I know I'd like to do something **unique.** I just don't want to do something **commonplace.**
Scott:	That's **odd.** I've had the same thoughts. Of course, I want to be well known in my field, whatever it is.
Regina:	Naturally. And don't forget, known for your research and **vital** discoveries.
Scott:	Of course! Nothing **petty** and **trivial** for us.
Regina:	That's right. Fame and fortune!
Scott:	Yes!
Regina:	Meanwhile, what do you say we get ourselves an ice cream cone?
Scott:	Great idea.
Regina:	Now what shall I have, chocolate, vanilla, strawberry? Such a difficult decision.

 EXERCISE 2

Work with a partner, with a group, or alone to answer the following questions.

1. What is Regina doing?

Task

Write the two kinds of thinking verbs Regina is using. What other thinking verbs do you know?

2. Is thinking about the future unusual for Scott?

Task

Find another word in the conversation that is similar in meaning to "familiar."

3. What kinds of decisions will Regina have to make?

Task

Find another word in the passage that means "important."

4. What kind of thing would Regina like to do?

Task

What is the opposite of the word "unique"? What words in the conversation mean "not important"? What words in the conversation are related to "thinking"?

5. Scott says, "That's odd." What does "odd" mean?

Task

Name two things that are odd to you.

6. What does Scott want to be in his field?

A. Thinking and Remembering

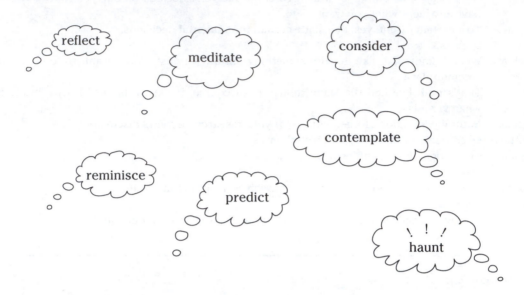

1. **to assume** = to take as fact with no proof; to suppose.

   Ex. I assume you will be home about seven tonight.

2. **to reminisce** = to remember or talk about the past in a pleasant way.

   Ex. Old people often reminisce about the days of their youth.

3. **to haunt** = to be in your thoughts, usually in an unpleasant way.

   Ex. The horrors he saw during the war haunted him.

4. **to reflect (on)** = to think over very carefully.

   Ex. He reflected for a moment before answering the question.

5. **to contemplate** = to think about deeply for a long time.

   Ex. He looked at the view from his window and contemplated his next move.

6. **to meditate** = to think deeply, concentrating on one matter. It is especially used in religion.

   Ex. The priest wanted to be alone and meditate before giving a decision.

7. **to predict** = tell beforehand.

   Ex. Weather reporters usually try to predict the weather as accurately as possible.

8. **to consider** = to think of carefully or in a certain way.

   Ex. Mozart was considered to be a great composer in his time.

9. **to conceive (of)** = think of; to imagine.

   Ex. It's hard to conceive what an earthquake greater than 8.0 on the Richter scale can do.

10. **to speculate** = to think about something in a way that is not serious because of a lack of facts.

    Ex. With constant changes in the government, it was only possible to speculate what would happen.

EXERCISE 1

Circle T if the sentence is TRUE and F if the sentence is FALSE.

1. To reflect means to think about something very carefully.　　　　　T　　F
2. To contemplate is to think about something for a long time.　　　　T　　F
3. To predict is to say something will happen before it does.　　　　T　　F
4. To haunt is to remember pleasant dreams.　　　　　　　　　　T　　F
5. To consider is to think of with care.　　　　　　　　　　　　T　　F
6. To reminisce is to recall the past with fear.　　　　　　　　　T　　F
7. To conceive of is to imagine.　　　　　　　　　　　　　　　T　　F
8. To assume is to think deeply and seriously.　　　　　　　　　T　　F

EXERCISE 2

Complete the sentences with the correct answer.

1. They refused to _____ my request to join the club.
   a. meditate　　　　　　　b. reflect　　　　　　　c. consider

2. His grandfather would often _____ about the time he was a young and famous athletic star.
   a. conceive　　　　　　　b. predict　　　　　　　c. reminisce

3. It is hard to _____ moving after twenty years in the same house.
   a. contemplate　　　　　b. speculate　　　　　　c. reminisce

4. Some sportsmen _____ to relax before a contest.
   a. meditate　　　　　　　b. predict　　　　　　　c. conceive

5. Now that he was alone he could _____ his past.
   a. predict　　　　　　　b. reflect on　　　　　　c. haunt

6. A billion ounces of gold is more wealth than most of us can _____.
   a. assume　　　　　　　b. meditate　　　　　　c. conceive of

7. He is my friend so I _____ that he is innocent.
   a. assume　　　　　　　b. predict　　　　　　　c. reminisce

8. The car crash still _____ me after ten years.
   a. considers　　　　　　b. haunts　　　　　　　c. meditates

9. Some people think that they can _____ the future.

   a. predict   b. reminisce   c. haunt

10. We can only _____ when the next earthquake will be.

    a. predict   b. reminisce   c. speculate

B. Important and Not Important

fundamental	vital	petty
indispensable	essential	trivial
significant	crucial	mere
	drastic	

1. **fundamental** = the base upon which a system is built and supported.

   Ex.   The constitution is the fundamental law of the United States.

2. **essential** = something belongs to the nature of something and therefore cannot be removed without destroying it.

   Ex.   Without the bare essentials of life a person will not survive.

3. **vital** = something necessary for the existence of a thing.

   Ex.   It is vital that the witness testifies in court.

4. **indispensable** = something that is too important or necessary to be without.

   Ex.   Nurses are indispensable in a hospital.

5. **crucial** = something very important which helps to decide the future. It is used in a crisis situation.

   Ex.   What we decide in the next few minutes is crucial because it will affect our lives.

6. **drastic** = rapid, harsh, and extreme action.

   Ex.   Drastic measures were taken by the government to control the rate of inflation.

7. **significant** = something important that has a meaning to the person who says it and those who hear it.

   Ex.   His speech on this sad occasion was very significant to us all.

8. **petty** = something of the least importance by comparison to other things.

   Ex.   I am tired of your petty excuses for being late.

9. **trivial** = something not important and very common and therefore not worth considering.

   Ex.   He occupied himself with trivial things because of his fear of dealing with important matters.

10. **mere** = no more than; emphasizes how limited a thing is.

    Ex.   What do you expect? He's a mere child.

EXERCISE 1

Circle T if the sentence is TRUE and F if the sentence is FALSE.

1.	Drastic means quick and hard.	T	F
2.	Something vital is necessary for it to survive.	T	F
3.	Something trivial is most important.	T	F
4.	The main support or idea behind something is fundamental to it.	T	F
5.	Mere means something is more than it appears.	T	F
6.	Something essential cannot be removed without destroying the whole.	T	F
7.	Indispensable means you can throw it away.	T	F
8.	Something petty is very important.	T	F
9.	Crucial can describe an important decision that needs to be taken affecting the future.	T	F
10.	Something significant has an important meaning to everyone concerned.	T	F

EXERCISE 2

Complete the sentences with the correct answer.

1. The bank loan was _____ to the project.

    a. indispensable   b. drastic   c. significant

2. A tornado requires _____ action by people in its path.

    a. mere   b. crucial   c. drastic

3. The _____ idea of capitalism is a free market economy.

    a. fundamental   b. vital   c. significant

4. It is stupid to get upset over _____ mistakes.

    a. essential   b. trivial   c. drastic

5. To take the exam now or to wait a year is a _____ decision.

    a. drastic   b. mere   c. crucial

6. His speech was _____ to all the audience, who would lose their jobs in the layoffs.

    a. fundamental   b. petty   c. significant

7. Their latest proposal is a _____ bluff.

    a. mere   b. petty   c. trivial

8. A/An _____ part of being a hero is not thinking before you take action.

    a. vital   b. petty   c. essential

9. When there are so many important things to be done, why does she insist on

so many _____ distractions?

   a. drastic   b. petty   c. vital

10. It is _____ that you get this message to Jim, or we will lose the account.

   a. vital   b. indispensable   c. significant

C. Usual and Unusual

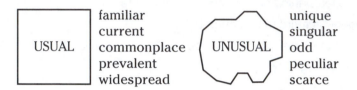

1. **familiar** = similar to what one knows; known or seen by everyone.

   Ex. When he talked about the problems in his country, they were quite familiar to us.

2. **current** = existing widely. It is usually used with fashion, language, practices and things which are constantly changing. It also means new, or recent if no other time is mentioned.

   Ex. There is an article on American slang in the current issue of *English Language Magazine*.

3. **commonplace** = found everywhere and usually implies that it is not very interesting or special.

   Ex. Car thefts are commonplace in this city.

4. **unique** = being the only one of its kind.

   Ex. Each man's fingerprint is unique.

5. **singular** = different from any other of its kind and suggests some kind of strangeness.

   Ex. Upon catching the snake I experienced a singular feeling I cannot describe.

6. **prevalent** = something that exists most of the time in some place.

   Ex. Malaria is prevalent in hot, swampy areas.

7. **widespread** = found in many places.

   Ex. The disease that attacked the leaves of the trees could not be controlled and soon became widespread.

8. **odd** = that which is not usual or normal.

   Ex. I don't know what kind of job he does but he leaves his house at odd hours.

9. **peculiar** = having a special distinctiveness in quality or character that is not pleasing.

   Ex. This flower has a peculiar smell.

10. **scarce** = hard to get or find.

   Ex. Because of intensive farming, certain wild birds have become scarce.

EXERCISE 1

Circle T if the sentence is TRUE and F if the sentence is FALSE.

1.	Something that is odd is not normal.	T	F
2.	Something current is not up-to-date.	T	F
3.	If a thing is widespread it is found everywhere.	T	F
4.	Something scarce is frightening.	T	F
5.	Things that are commonplace are not very interesting and can be found everywhere.	T	F
6.	Singular means usual and like everything else.	T	F
7.	Something peculiar has a special, unpleasant aspect.	T	F
8.	A unique object has no equal.	T	F

EXERCISE 2

Complete the sentences with the correct answer.

1. The price of fruit increased because it was _____.

   a. prevalent   b. odd   c. scarce

2. His wooden leg gave him a _____ appearance.

   a. singular   b. scarce   c. widespread

3. Disease is _____ in many poor countries.

   a. prevalent   b. current   c. peculiar

4. The man frightened me with his _____ smile.

   a. widespread   b. familiar   c. peculiar

5. The handmade car sold for a million because it was _____.

   a. unique   b. scarce   c. commonplace

6. The _____ fashion is the same as my grandmother's!

   a. familiar   b. odd   c. current

7. The tune the band was playing sounded _____.

   a. prevalent   b. familiar   c. widespread

8. Unfortunately, the latest film just tells a _____ story.

   a. commonplace   b. widespread   c. unique

9. Panic was _____ after the dam burst.

   a. scarce   b. widespread   c. singular

10. To stand on your head at a party is _____ behavior.

    a. commonplace   b. odd   c. current

Test on Thought and Communication

Choose the answer that could best replace the underlined word without changing the meaning of the sentence.

1. Hypertension is one of the most <u>widespread</u> and potentially dangerous diseases.

   (A) colossal   (B) popular

   (C) common   (D) scattered

2. The gravitational forces of the sun and the moon are <u>fundamental</u> in causing ocean tides.

   (A) unique   (B) essential

   (C) odd   (D) current

3. Jazz appeared as a <u>unique</u> form of American music in the 1920s.

   (A) obscure   (B) scarce

   (C) vital   (D) singular

4. In the learning situation, exposure to language and motivation are <u>crucial</u> factors in language learning.

   (A) moderate   (B) vital

   (C) mere   (D) drastic

5. Gregor Mendel <u>conceived of</u> the laws of heredity from observing the growth of peas.

   (A) assumed   (B) reminisced of

   (C) thought of   (D) meditated about

6. Harriet Beecher Stowe was an <u>obscure</u> writer until the publication of *Uncle Tom's Cabin*.

   (A) anonymous   (B) unknown

   (C) infamous   (D) eminent

7. After years of work and <u>contemplation</u>, the Native American Sequoyah single-handedly invented a written language for his people.

   (A) worry   (B) sickness

   (C) deep thought   (D) loneliness

8. Although the <u>prevalent</u> attitude toward tarantulas is one of fear, they actually benefit humans by controlling the insect population.

   (A) petty   (B) popular

   (C) essential   (D) unusual

9. Laura Scudder's <u>singular</u> concept of prepackaged potato chips made her a legend in the food industry.

   (A) unique   (B) familiar

   (C) unknown   (D) unappreciated

10. Apples not only contain several <u>essential</u> vitamins but have been proven to aid digestion and help keep teeth healthy and clean.

   (A) extra   (B) common

   (C) unusual   (D) important

CHAPTER 7

Theme Grouping:
Feelings and Sensations

Reading Practice

Read the following passage.

Most people think of algae as the dirty green layer on a fish pond. But another kind of algae known as kelp or seaweed has become an important part of the American diet. Without being the least bit **daring**, Americans eat seaweed by the ton. That's because they usually don't know it! From the sweet **flavored** jelly coming out of a doughnut, to a crisp pile of **savory** onion rings, there's more seaweed in food than most people know.

Algin, a substance extracted from ground-up seaweed, has the unique ability to make liquids more solid. Thus it is used in hundreds of prepared foods, from ice cream to salad dressing.

The entire U.S. kelp harvest comes from the coastal waters off Southern California. Ships move through huge kelp beds and take two or three feet off the top of the 100-foot plants. More than 56,000 tons of wet seaweed are harvested each year. The harvesters are by no means being **ruthless**, however. Cutting the kelp actually helps it to grow, thereby ensuring a constant supply of seaweed for hungry Americans!

 ## EXERCISE 1

Work with a partner, with a group, or alone to answer the following questions.

1. When Americans eat seaweed, how do they act?

Task

What do you think "daring" means? What is the opposite of "daring"? Give an example of a daring person. Say why.

2. In what kinds of foods can you find seaweed?

Task

What do you think "savory" means? Name two other foods that are savory.

3. By cutting the kelp each year, are Americans being ruthless?

Task

What do you think "ruthless" means? What other word is similar to "ruthless"? Give an example of a ruthless person. Say why.

Conversation Practice

Read the following conversation.

Roberta:	Pardon me. Am I on the right trail to Eagle Lake?
John:	Yes, it's less than a mile to the Eagle Crest. From there it's about one-half mile to the lake.
Roberta:	Thank goodness. I was beginning to think I was lost.
John:	I thought you were looking a little **apprehensive**. My group is hiking to Eagle Lake too. Would you like to join us?
Roberta:	Oh, thank you. You're very **considerate**. It seems I'm not as **bold** as I thought I would be.
John:	Well, you should never hike alone on this mountain. No matter how **courageous** you are, it's best to hike with one or more people.
Roberta:	Yes, it was foolish of me, I know. I'll never do it again.
John:	Why don't you sit on this log for a minute and rest until my friends catch up? How about some lemonade? It's a little **sour** but its cold.

Roberta: Thank you. I'd like that. You're very **generous**. I'm glad that I ran into you today!
John: Oh, here come my friends! Are you ready to go on?
Roberta: Ready!

 ## EXERCISE 2

Work with a partner, with a group, or alone to answer the following questions.

1. How did John think Roberta was looking?

Task

Why do you think she looked that way? How would you feel if you were lost? What do you think is the meaning of "apprehensive"? Describe a situation when you feel apprehensive.

2. What does Roberta think about John when he asks her to join his group?

Task

Why does she think this? Give another word to describe this kind of person. What is the word for the opposite of this kind of person?

3. What does Roberta think about herself?

Task

What do you think this word means? Find another word in the conversation that is similar.

4. What is the lemonade like?

Task

What other foods are "sour"?

5. What does Roberta think about John when he offers her the lemonade?

Task

What is the opposite of this word? Who do you think is generous? Say why.

A. Kindness and Unkindness

benevolent  benign
considerate humane
generous

mean  selfish
ruthless spiteful
merciless

1. **benevolent** = kind and wanting to do good and help others.

    Ex. She was a benevolent lady who gave most of what she had to help orphans.

2. **benign** = kind and friendly. When used about a disease, it means it is not dangerous.

    Ex. He was pleased to find that the tumor on his head was benign.

3. **humane** = showing kindness and compassion. It is usually used about the ways others are treated.

    Ex. On their return, the hostages said they had been treated in a humane way.

4. **considerate** = thoughtful of others, concerned with others' feelings.

    Ex. It was very considerate of her to come and take care of me when I was sick.

5. **generous** = kind and ready to give money, help, time, etc.

    Ex. We could not forget his generous offer of assistance.

6. **selfish** = wanting everything for oneself.

    Ex. My sister is so selfish. She never lets anyone watch what they want on television. It's always what she wants.

7. **mean** = not generous or kind. It is also used for someone who likes to hurt.

    Ex. He always plays the part of the bad guy in the movies because he has a mean-looking face.

8. **spiteful** = wanting to do evil, usually in a small way. Also, wanting to get even with someone for a real or unreal reason.

    Ex. Just to be spiteful, the little girl destroyed her sister's doll.

9. **merciless** = being able to be cruel without worrying about it; having no kindness of heart.

    Ex. The enemy was merciless and killed a village full of women and children.

10. **ruthless** = having no pity or kindness.

    Ex. Everyone knew the commander was a ruthless person who would do anything to gain power.

 EXERCISE 1

Circle T if the sentence is TRUE and F if the sentence is FALSE.

1. Someone who is selfish wants it all for himself.	T	F
2. A merciless person does not feel sad to be cruel.	T	F
3. To be benign is to be kind and friendly.	T	F
4. A generous person takes everything he can get.	T	F
5. Ruthless means unable to be cruel.	T	F

6. A mean person is kind and generous.   T   F
7. A benevolent person wants to do good and be kind.   T   F
8. Spiteful behavior is kind and gentle.   T   F

EXERCISE 2

Complete the sentences with the correct answer.

1. They say that people who treat animals in a _____ way are kind to people too.

   a. selfish   b. merciless   c. humane

2. A _____ businessman is one who destroys his competitors.

   a. generous   b. spiteful   c. ruthless

3. A _____ person hurts you in little ways.

   a. spiteful   b. merciless   c. benign

4. The king was a good man and a _____ leader of his people.

   a. selfish   b. merciless   c. benign

5. She was a _____ tennis player and never gave her opponent even the smallest

   chance.

   a. merciless   b. spiteful   c. selfish

6. A _____ man, he always gave money to the poor.

   a. ruthless   b. selfish   c. generous

7. She was so _____ of others that she always served her guests their favorite foods

   even if she did not like them.

   a. mean   b. considerate   c. merciless

8. He is so _____ he will not even give you one french fry.

   a. benign   b. generous   c. selfish

9. The sick and dying loved the _____ lady who came to visit.

   a. benevolent   b. mean   c. ruthless

10. It is _____ to tie your grandmother's shoelaces together.

    a. considerate   b. mean   c. selfish

B. Fear and Courage

 scared
timid
apprehensive
cowardly
petrified

 daring
bold
intrepid
courageous
audacious

1. **scary** = making one afraid.

    Ex. With all those strange noises, this house is scary at night.

2. **timid** = having fear, not having courage.

    Ex. He's a very timid person and will neither speak out nor take a risk.

3. **apprehensive** = a state of mind that is fearful, but the fear may have some reason.

    Ex. With the tense situation between the two countries, people were apprehensive of war.

4. **cowardly** = unable to face danger because the person is afraid and lacks courage.

    Ex. His cowardly behavior made everyone avoid him.

5. **petrified** = in a state of great shock or fear, like turning into stone.

    Ex. I was petrified when I saw the man standing there with a gun in his hand.

6. **bold** = having courage.

    Ex. He was a bold man to cross that dangerous territory with only a knife to defend himself.

7. **courageous** = showing bravery.

    Ex. He was given a medal for his courageous act that saved the lives of five men.

8. **daring** = taking risks in challenging situations.

    Ex. His idea for a new type of television commercial seems very daring, and may even shock people.

9. **intrepid** = ready to meet danger again and again.

    Ex. The couple, intrepid explorers, went into the Amazon.

10. **audacious** = daring or brave to a point which is excessive.

    Ex. He was audacious enough to tell the committee that they were fools.

 EXERCISE **1**

Circle T if the sentence is TRUE and F if the sentence is FALSE.

1. Daring is taking risks when it is easy to do so.	T	F
2. If you are too afraid to move you are petrified.	T	F
3. Timid is not having the time to be afraid.	T	F
4. If you are bold you have courage.	T	F
5. Apprehensive is being afraid in advance.	T	F

6. A cowardly person runs toward danger.   T   F

7. Audacious means being extremely brave or daring.   T   F

8. Something scary makes you afraid.   T   F

9. A courageous person does brave things.   T   F

10. Intrepid means ready to run away again and again.   T   F

EXERCISE 2

Complete the sentences with the correct answer.

1. It was a _____ move to say no to the boss.

   a. cowardly   b. timid   c. bold

2. To swim across the river at night was _____ of him.

   a. audacious   b. scary   c. timid

3. It was _____ of her to pull the children from the fire.

   a. intrepid   b. courageous   c. apprehensive

4. It was _____ of her to run and hide.

   a. intrepid   b. cowardly   c. audacious

5. Riding on the back of his new motorcycle was _____.

   a. intrepid   b. petrified   c. scary

6. Many people are _____ of flying.

   a. apprehensive   b. audacious   c. cowardly

7. If you are _____ in business you will not succeed.

   a. audacious   b. timid   c. scary

8. It will take a very _____ plan to surprise them.

   a. apprehensive   b. scary   c. daring

9. The _____ salesman covered every inch of his territory.

   a. intrepid   b. apprehensive   c. petrified

10. When the captain announced he was turning the aircraft back to the airport, we were all

   _____.

   a. intrepid   b. courageous   c. petrified

C. Types of Taste

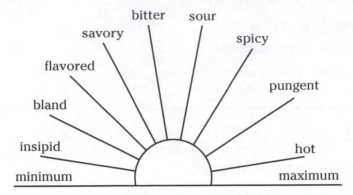

1. **bland** = without much taste.

    Ex. Boiled potatoes with nothing on them may seem bland to many people.

2. **insipid** = lacking a strong taste; having a weak and watery taste.

    Ex. I remember eating food that was insipid at that hospital.

3. **flavored** = having a substance that gives taste.

    Ex. The children enjoy chocolate-flavored ice cream.

4. **savory** = having a pleasant taste that is not sweet.

    Ex. For those who don't like sweets like cakes and cookies there are savory things like salty crackers and cheese.

5. **sour** = having a taste that is not sweet such as in milk that has gone bad.

    Ex. These grapes are very sour.

6. **bitter** = having a sharp taste that is not sweet as in coffee without sugar.

    Ex. This medication has a very bitter taste.

7. **spicy** = containing natural additives usually in the form of powder which have a strong taste.

    Ex. There's a spicy fruit drink made with cinnamon and cloves.

8. **pungent** = having a strong, sharp taste or smell that often stings.

    Ex. Indian curry often has a pungent taste.

9. **hot** = containing natural additives which are very strong and give a burning sensation to the mouth.

    Ex. Many Mexican dishes contain hot chili peppers.

 EXERCISE 1

Circle T if the sentence is TRUE and F if the sentence is FALSE.

1. Spicy means too cold to taste.	T	F
2. Something flavored is what you like best.	T	F
3. Hot means containing things that give a burning taste.	T	F
4. Something bitter has no sweetness and is sharp to taste.	T	F

5. Bland food has a very strong taste.   T   F
6. Something pungent has a strong, sharp taste or smell that stings.   T   F
7. Savory means having a taste which is not sweet but salty or spicy and pleasant. T   F
8. Something insipid has little or no taste and can be weak and watery.   T   F

EXERCISE 2

Complete the sentences with the correct answer.

1. The strong garlic sauce had a _____ flavor.
   a. sour   b. bland   c. pungent

2. Many types of sausage are made _____ by adding pepper.
   a. hot   b. bitter   c. bland

3. The guests enjoyed _____ snacks at the reception.
   a. savory   b. insipid   c. bitter

4. With no sugar or raisins, oatmeal is very _____.
   a. spicy   b. flavored   c. bland

5. Yogurt has a naturally _____ taste.
   a. savory   b. sour   c. hot

6. Aspirins without water taste _____ if you chew them.
   a. bitter   b. spicy   c. pungent

7. Do you like duck _____ with orange?
   a. bitter   b. bland   c. flavored

8. I like _____ food but it does not always like me!
   a. spicy   b. insipid   c. bland

9. There was so much water in the soup it tasted _____.
   a. spicy   b. insipid   c. bitter

Test on Feelings and Sensations

Choose the answer that could best replace the underlined word without changing the meaning of the sentence.

1. Dorothea Dix crusaded for the <u>humane</u> treatment of the mentally ill.
   (A) compassionate   (B) ruthless
   (C) audacious   (D) apprehensive

2. Bats are <u>timid</u> creatures.

   (A) shy

   (B) audacious

   (C) petrified

   (D) considerable

3. Paul Revere <u>daringly</u> rode through the New England countryside to warn the colonists.

   (A) benevolently

   (B) courageously

   (C) apprehensively

   (D) mercilessly

4. Ketchup was developed from a tasty, <u>spicy</u> Chinese sauce made of pickled fish and shellfish in the 17th century.

   (A) insipid

   (B) flavored

   (C) bland

   (D) sour

5. The largest <u>petrified</u> forest in the world is in northern Arizona.

   (A) generous

   (B) intrepid

   (C) stone

   (D) insipid

6. A <u>benign</u> lesion usually has a regular border.

   (A) humane

   (B) petrified

   (C) congenial

   (D) harmless

7. Acorns are <u>bitter</u> to taste.

   (A) sharp

   (B) sour

   (C) acrid

   (D) intrepid

8. Robert Peary, an <u>intrepid</u> explorer, was the first to reach the North Pole.

   (A) daring

   (B) ruthless

   (C) audacious

   (D) insipid

9. The <u>benevolent</u> Emma Willard started women's education by opening a school in her home in 1814.

   (A) apprehensive

   (B) merciless

   (C) spiteful

   (D) kind

10. It took a great deal of <u>courage</u> for the early explorers to set sail on uncharted seas.

    (A) foolishness

    (B) bravery

    (C) benevolence

    (D) timidity

11. Many of America's parks and monuments have been made possible by the <u>generous</u> donations of its citizens.

    (A) kindhearted

    (B) unwanted

    (C) selfish

    (D) meaningless

12. <u>Flavored</u> vinegars are produced especially for cooking, but white vinegars have a number of household uses.

    (A) bland

    (B) bitter

    (C) concentrated

    (D) special tasting

CHAPTER 8

Idioms and
Confusing Words

There are thousands of idioms in English. The 100 idioms in this section are some of the most common idioms you are likely to encounter in the short dialogues and conversations in the Listening Comprehension section of the TOEFL® test.

In this section we will also look at some confusing words in English. Some of these are expressions with MAKE and DO, and others are words which sound similar or have similar meanings.

Conversation Practice

Read the following dialogue.

> Linda: Are you going to the movies with us tonight, Mark?
>
> Mark: No, I'm afraid that going to the movies is **out of the question** until I've finished my term paper.

 EXERCISE 1

Work with a partner, with a group, or alone to answer the following questions.

1. From the conversation, do you think Mark will go to to the movies?
2. What do you think the idiom "out of the question" means?

Task

What is "out of the question" for you?

Conversation Practice

Read the following dialogue.

> Donald: Do you think we'll see whooping cranes on our bird-watching trip?
>
> Peter: It's not likely. Whooping cranes are an endangered species and sightings of them are **few and far between.**

 EXERCISE 2

Work with a partner, with a group, or alone to answer the following questions.

1. From the conversation, do you think they will see whooping cranes?
2. What do you think the idiom "few and far between" means?

Task

Tell about something that happens that is "few and far between."

Conversation Practice

Read the following dialogue.

> June: How did Tom do on his physics exam today?
>
> Alan: I don't know, but he studied hard so I **have a hunch** he did well.

EXERCISE 3

Work with a partner, with a group, or alone to answer the following questions.

1. From the conversation do you think that Tom did well on his exam?

2. What do you think the idiom "have a hunch" means?

Task

What do you have a hunch about?

Conversation Practice

Read the following conversation.

Joan:	Hello, Paul. I didn't think I'd **run into** you today.
Paul:	My plans to go skiing this weekend **fell through.**
Joan:	In that case, why don't you **drop by** my house for dinner tonight?
Paul:	Thanks, I'd love to.
Joan:	Three of my girlfriends from school are coming too.
Paul:	Three girls! But I'll feel like a **fish out of water.**
Joan:	Oh, come on. It's time you **made** some new friends. Besides, you can help us **do** our homework afterwards.
Paul:	Aha! I knew there had to be **another** reason why you asked me to dinner.
Joan:	I have to admit that besides the fact that you're my favorite cousin, we really could use your help.
Paul:	All right then. But just remember that you owe me a favor.
Joan:	I'll remember. Thanks, Paul. See you at six.

 EXERCISE 4

Work with a partner, with a group, or alone to answer the following questions.

1. Was Joan running when she met Paul?

Task

From the conversation what do you think the idiom "run into" means? Whom did you run into recently?

2. What happened to Paul's plans to go skiing?

Task

In your answer above, what do the verb and the preposition mean separately? Is this the meaning in the conversation? From the conversation what do you think this idiom means?

3. Why do you think Paul will feel like a "fish out of water"?

Task

From the conversation what do you think the idiom "a fish out of water" means? Describe two situations when a person can feel like "a fish out of water."

4. What does Joan think it's time for Paul to do?

Task

Give three expressions with the verb *make*.

5. What can Paul help Jean and her friends do?

Task

Give three expressions with the verb *do*.

6. Did Paul know why Joan asked him to dinner?

Task

Is there a difference between *another* and *other?* Discuss and explain.

STRATEGIES

- Listening to conversations and discussions whether it be in real life or on television or in movies will help you familiarize yourself with idiomatic expressions. It is important that you develop an "ear" for the use of idioms and remember situations where they are used.

- There are different ways of remembering idioms. Some people prefer to memorize idioms. Other people remember by associating the word in an idiom with a visual picture like an animal or object.

EXAMPLES

- After you remember the idiom, it is important to know in which situation and with whom you can use it. For example, if you do not know the answer to your teacher's question and you reply "Search me," this may not be the appropriate answer when talking to a teacher. However, for the TOEFL you do not need to use idiomatic expressions, you only need to recognize them.

- If you do not know or understand the idiom, look for clues in the context of the conversation.

EXAMPLES

"You look pale today. Are you feeling under the weather?"

The word "pale" gives you a clue that the idiom "under the weather" means "not feeling well."

Woman: I just broke my mother's favorite vase.

Man: You'll be in hot water.

The woman's comment about breaking her mother's vase helps you understand that the idiom "in hot water" means "in trouble."

A. Idioms

1. **above all**—most importantly
2. **as a matter of fact**—in fact, to speak the truth
3. **as a rule**—generally; normally
4. **be about to**—be ready to; be on the point of doing something
5. **be an old hand**—be an experienced person
6. **be fed up with**—be out of patience with
7. **be on one's own**—live independently
8. **be on the safe side**—take no chances
9. **be out of something**—have no longer in supply
10. **be tired of**—be bored with, frustrated with

 EXERCISE 1

Complete the sentences or dialogues with idioms from the list. Change the verb to the correct tense when necessary.

1. A: Have you started studying for your biology test?

   B: Not yet, I was just _____ _____.

2. Although it's warm today, I think you should take a sweater, just to _____

   _____ _____ _____

   _____ .

3. Don't worry. I can change your tire. I'm an _____ _____ at it.

4. I have several goals in life, but _____ _____ I want to be well

   educated.

5. I wish I could offer you some coffee, but I'm _____ _____ it.

6. A: I heard you just got your own apartment.

   B: That's right, I'm finally going to live _____ _____

   _____ .

7. A: What do you usually do on weekends, Fred?

   B: _____ _____ _____ I stay at home, but next

   weekend I'm going to San Francisco with a friend.

8. I'll be happy when the new season of TV programs begins. I'm _____

   _____ watching reruns.

Idioms

11. **be up to one's ears**—be extremely busy
12. **be up to someone**—be a person's responsibility
13. **be out of the question**—be unacceptable, impossible
14. **bite off more than one can chew**—take on more than one can handle
15. **break the ice**—begin to be friendly with people one doesn't know
16. **break the news**—inform or give bad news
17. **brush up on**—improve one's knowledge of something through study
18. **bump into**—meet unexpectedly
19. **by and large**—in general
20. **by heart**—by memory

 ## EXERCISE 2

Circle the best answer.

1. If Sean had to break the news to Mario about his damaged fender, Mario
   a. already knew about it.
   b. wouldn't be unhappy.
   c. would be hearing about it for the first time.

2. If Hans bumped into Sally at the mall yesterday, he
   a. didn't expect to see her.
   b. had an appointment with her.
   c. tried to knock her down.

3. If you're up to your ears with homework, you
   a. don't have much to do.
   b. have a lot to do.
   c. can't wait to get started.

4. Peter started talking to Amanda about the weather, just to break the ice. Peter
   a. spilled ice on Amanda.
   b. acted in a cold manner.
   c. tried to be friendly.

5. If you had to learn a list of dates by heart for your history exam, you
   a. had to memorize them.
   b. had to write them down.
   c. had to feel good about them.

6. Alfredo looked down the expert ski slope and realized he had bitten off more than he could chew. Alfredo
   a. had chosen a ski area beyond his ability.
   b. knew he could easily ski down the slope.
   c. had his mouth full of food.

7. If Estelle brushed up on her French before her trip to France, she
   a. made some plans.
   b. did some cleaning.
   c. did some studying.

8. If your teacher has told you it is out of the question for you to turn in your term paper late, you
   a. must turn in your paper on time.
   b. have extra time to work on your paper.
   c. don't have any more questions to ask your teacher.

Idioms

21. **by all means**—absolutely, definitely
22. **by no means**—in no way
23. **cheer up**—be happy
24. **come down with**—become sick with
25. **come up with**—think of
26. **count on**—depend upon
27. **count out**—eliminate
28. **die down**—become quiet, become less
29. **do without**—manage without something
30. **drop by**—visit informally; pay a short visit

 EXERCISE 3

Write C for the correct sentences and I for the incorrect sentences.

_____ 1. A: Are you coming to my party tomorrow?

B: Yes, you can count on me.

_____ 2. I'll be home this afternoon. Drop by anytime.

_____ 3. I tried to think of an excuse, but I couldn't come down with one fast enough.

_____ 4. Mary was depressed so I took her to a funny movie and she cheered up.

_____ 5. I forgot my notebook for class but I think I can do without it.

_____ 6. The wind was very strong at first but after a while it counted out.

_____ 7. A: You're looking a bit tired today.

B: Well, I think I'm coming up with the flu.

_____ 8. A: May I share this bench with you?

B: By no means. You're very welcome to sit here.

Idioms

31. **every other**—alternate
32. **fall behind**—lag; fail to accomplish something on time
33. **fall through**—fail to happen or be completed
34. **far cry from**—completely different from; a long way
35. **feel like**—have a desire or wish for
36. **feel up to**—feel well enough to or be capable of
37. **few and far between**—not happening often; rare
38. **figure out**—determine; reason out by thinking
39. **fish out of water**—out of one's element or natural environment
40. **for good**—permanently; forever

 EXERCISE 4

Complete the sentences or dialogues with idioms from the list. Change the verb to the correct tense when necessary.

1. I know you haven't been feeling well lately, but do you _____

   _____ _____ a drive today?

2. I don't have physics every day. I have it _____ _____ day.

3. A: Are you going to be staying in the United States for a while?

   B: Yes, I'm here _____ _____ .

4. Michael felt like _____ _____ _____

   _____ _____ because he was the only man in a room full of

   women.

5. A: Let's stop and take a rest.

   B: No, we'd better keep walking or we'll _____ _____ the other

   hikers.

6. Roberto, could you help me, please? I can't _____ _____ how to

   put my little sister's new bicycle together.

7. Our plans to go to the mountains _____ _____ when I got sick.

8. A: What do you want to do today?

   B: I _____ _____ going to the beach.

Idioms

41. **for the time being**—for now; temporarily
42. **get rid of**—give something away; sell, destroy or throw away something
43. **get the ball rolling**—start something; make a beginning
44. **get the hang of**—understand; learn
45. **give a hand**—help
46. **go without saying**—understood; clear without needing to be stated
47. **hang on**—keep hold of; persevere; keep doing something
48. **hard to come by**—difficult to obtain
49. **have a heart**—have kind feelings; be understanding
50. **have a hunch**—have an idea based on feelings rather than reason

 EXERCISE 5

Circle the best answer.

1. After many hours with her tennis coach, Yolanda finally got the hang of serving. Yolanda
   a. learned how to serve.   b. hung up her tennis racket
   c. still doesn't know how to serve.

2. If the special edition of a book is hard to come by, it
   a. can be found in almost any bookstore.   b. is a hardcover edition.
   c. is difficult to find.

3. If Johannes finally got rid of his old football, he
   a. is saving it for the future.   b. no longer has it.
   c. loaned it to a friend for a short while.

4. If you have a hunch that Melinda will be at the party tonight, you
   a. know she'll be there.   b. think she'll be there.
   c. wonder if she'll be there.

5. If Mai Lin was the one who got the ball rolling on your group science project, she
   a. put off working on the project.   b. rolled a ball around as part of the project.
   c. started work on the project.

6. If you gave your neighbor a hand with her groceries, you
   a. helped her.   b. avoided her.
   c. shook hands with her.

7. Stanley used a bit of wire to fix his car door for the time being. Stanley
   a. permanently fixed the car door.   b. temporarily fixed the car door.
   c. didn't know how to fix the car door.

8. If Gerard is hanging on to an old clock, he
   a. is keeping it.   b. is holding it in his hands.
   c. is going to throw it away.

Idioms

51. **hop to it**—get started on something quickly
52. **hit it off**—get along well with someone
53. **ill at ease**—uncomfortable
54. **in hot water**—in trouble
55. **in the dark**—keep someone without knowledge; keep information from someone
56. **in the long run**—looking toward the future; eventually
57. **ins and outs**—all the details; the various parts and difficulties to be seen
58. **iron out**—remove the difficulties or find an answer for
59. **jump to conclusions**—arrive too quickly at a decision or opinion
60. **keep an eye on**—watch closely

 EXERCISE 6

Write C for the correct sentences and I for the incorrect sentences.

_____ 1. You may not like getting a flu shot now but in the dark it will be good for you.

_____ 2. Keep your eye on the children while I go to the store.

_____ 3. Before her friends arrived, she felt in hot water because she didn't know anyone in the room.

_____ 4. The minute he looked at the test he knew he was jumping to conclusions because he had not studied for it.

_____ 5. You'd better hit it off or you'll never be ready on time.

_____ 6. Reynaldo is an excellent tour guide because he knows all the ins and outs of traveling.

_____ 7. Don't worry about your misunderstanding with the manager. I'll get it all ironed out for you.

_____ 8. Sam started classes at a new school and was pleasantly surprised when he immediately kept an eye on his classmates.

Idioms

61. **keep one's fingers crossed**—wish that nothing goes wrong
62. **keep on one's toes**—be ready for action; prepared
63. **learn the ropes**—learn the rules and routines of a place or activity
64. **make ends meet**—to get just enough money for one's needs
65. **mean to**—intentional; on purpose
66. **might as well**—to have no strong reason not to
67. **next to nothing**—almost nothing; very inexpensive
68. **not to mention**—in addition
69. **off balance**—unaware; off guard
70. **on the go**—working or doing something all the time

 EXERCISE 7

Circle the best answer.

1. Carl and Monica are keeping their fingers crossed that the weather will be nice on their wedding day. They
   a. are wishing for nice weather.
   b. have been told the weather will be nice.
   c. don't really care about the weather.

2. If Leslie caught you off balance, he
   a. surprised you.
   b. stopped you from falling.
   c. played catch with you.

3. Norma paid next to nothing for her new purse. She
   a. paid a lot for it.
   b. got a bargain.
   c. got her purse for free.

4. If Kayla has learned the ropes on her new job, she
   a. has a lot to learn.
   b. has a job making ropes.
   c. knows her job.

5. Jamal decided to take an extra language course just to stay on his toes. Jamal
   a. wants to be prepared.
   b. likes to exercise.
   c. doesn't plan ahead.

6. If Julie earns just enough money to make ends meet, she
   a. earns more than she needs.
   b. doesn't earn enough to live on.
   c. earns just enough to pay her bills.

7. If the pitcher didn't mean to hit the batter, he
   a. did it on purpose.
   b. wasn't being a very good sport.
   c. didn't intend to do it.

8. If you're constantly on the go, you
   a. aren't very busy.
   b. are doing something all the time.
   c. have some bad habits.

Idioms

71. **on pins and needles**—nervous; anxious; full of anticipation
72. **on purpose**—deliberately; intentionally
73. **on the blink**—not working properly; broken
74. **on the right track**—thinking or doing something correctly
75. **on the tip of one's tongue**—to be about to remember something
76. **once in a blue moon**—rarely; almost never
77. **pick up the tab**—pay the bill or the cost of something
78. **piece of cake**—easy
79. **play by ear**—act spontaneously; without planning
80. **pull it off**—accomplish

 EXERCISE **8**

Complete the sentences or dialogues with idioms from the list. Change the verb to the correct tense when necessary.

1. Since Alberto does not like the ballet we only go _____ _____ _____ _____ _____.

2. A: Why didn't you take your car to school today?

   B: I couldn't drive it. It's _____ _____ _____.

3. A: Do you remember who starred in that movie?

   B: I know who it is, but I can't remember her name. It's _____ _____ _____ _____ _____ _____.

4. A: Let me help you with the check.

   B: No. Since it's your birthday I'll _____ _____ _____ _____.

5. A: How was the test? Was it easy?

   B: Oh yes. It was a _____ _____ _____.

6. A: Do you have plans for the holiday weekend?

   B: No. I'm going to _____ _____ _____.

7. I may not have my problem solved but at least I know I'm _____ _____ _____ _____.

8. I have all the tools for this job, but I'm still not sure I can _____ _____ _____.

Idioms

81. **pull one's leg**—make fun of someone in a playful way; make someone believe something that is not true
82. **quite a few**—many
83. **right away**—immediately
84. **run for office**—compete for an elected position
85. **save one's breath**—to keep silent because talking would not achieve anything
86. **say that again**—a saying that means: I agree completely
87. **stone's throw**—short distance
88. **search me**—an answer that means: I don't know
89. **serves one right**—is deserving of
90. **sleep on it**—think about something for a while

 EXERCISE 9

Write C for the correct sentences and I for the incorrect sentences.

_____ 1. A: I failed my math test.

B: Well, it pulls your leg since you didn't study.

_____ 2. A: Have you ever been to Yosemite National Park?

B: Yes, I've gone there quite a few times.

_____ 3. When she told me she'd won $25,000, I thought she was saving her breath.

_____ 4. We'll have to go to the bank right away as it will be closing very soon.

_____ 5. A: Do you live very far?

B: No. It's just a quite a few away.

_____ 6. Class elections are coming up and I've decided to search me.

_____ 7. A: I can't decide which television I want to buy.

B: Then why don't you sleep on it and come back tomorrow?

_____ 8. A: The weather is absolutely perfect today.

B: You can say that again!

Idioms

91. **straighten up**—clean up; make tidy
92. **take a break**—rest for a while; stop one's work or activity
93. **think nothing of it**—that's all right
94. **throw cold water on**—discourage; lessen enthusiasm for
95. **to say the least**—at the lowest estimate
96. **under the weather**—not feeling well
97. **well worth the trouble**—it deserves the inconvenience or trouble
98. **whole new ballgame**—an entirely different situation
99. **with flying colors**—succeed very well
100. **without a hitch**—without difficulty or delay

 EXERCISE 10

Complete the sentences or dialogues with idioms from the list. Change the verb to the correct tense when necessary.

1. I'm sorry I won't be able to go to the art exhibit with you tonight, but I'm feeling

   _____ _____ _____.

2. A: Did your presentation go well yesterday?

   B: Yes, there were no problems. Everything went smoothly _____

   _____ _____.

3. I am so excited about going out tonight. I hope you are not going to _____

   _____ _____ _____ my plans by saying you

   can't go.

4. I was so happy when I received my grades yesterday. I passed my courses

   _____ _____ _____

5. We're getting tired. Let's _____ _____ _____.

6. A: Boy, is your room a mess!

   B: I know. Mom told me I can't leave until I get it _____ _____.

7. A: Did you have a hard time finding grandmother's birthday present?

   B: Yes, but when I saw her expression when she opened it, I knew it was _____

   _____ _____ _____.

8. A: Thank you so much for helping me get my car started.

   B: _____ _____ _____ _____.

   It was no problem at all.

Test for Idioms

Circle the best answer.

1. M: I heard you have a part in the school play tonight.
   W: Yes, and I'm on pins and needles.
   How does the woman feel?

   a. Happy.   b. Angry.

   c. Nervous.   d. Confused.

2. W: Do you get pay raises where you work?
   M: Yes, but they are few and far between.
   What does the man mean?

   a. He gets lots of raises at his job.   b. There are no raises given where he works.

   c. They don't give raises very   d. He has to go far to get a raise.
      often where he works.

3. W: Have you made our plane reservations yet?
   M: No, I'm leaving it up to you.
   What does the man want the woman to do?

   a. Leave him alone.   b. Make the plane reservations.

   c. Let him make the reservations.   d. Get someone else to make the reservations.

4. M: I don't want that puppy in the house.
   W: Oh, have a heart.
   What does the woman mean?

   a. She wants the man to feel   b. She wants the man to hold
      sympathy for the puppy.   onto his heart.

   c. She wants the man to dislike the puppy.   d. She wants the man to ignore the puppy.

5. M: How was your blind date last night?
   W: We hit it off right away.
   What does the woman mean?

   a. She had a quarrel with her date.   b. She and her date left quickly.

   c. She and her date knocked   d. She and her date got along well.
      something down.

6. W: I should tell them they need more decorations.
   M: They never listen to anyone, so save your breath.
   What does the man want the woman to do?

   a. Not say anything.   b. Hold her breath.

   c. Make some suggestions.   d. Listen to the others.

7. M: I think something must be wrong because Vincent wasn't home when I called.
   W: Oh, you are always jumping to conclusions.
   What is the woman implying about the man?

   a. He is thoughtful about things.   b. He arrives at opinions too quickly.

   c. He's always jumping around.   d. He doesn't know how to make a decision.

8. M: I hope to be a well-known artist someday.
    W: Well, you're certainly on the right track.
    What does the woman's comment mean?

    a. She thinks the man is on a train.
    b. She thinks the man is right-handed.
    c. She thinks the man doesn't realize what he has to do.
    d. She thinks the man is doing what is necessary.

9. W: It's raining outside!
    M: Then why don't we stay in for the time being?
    What does the man mean?

    a. He doesn't want to go out at all.
    b. He wants to wait a while before going out.
    c. It's not time for them to go.
    d. He doesn't care to stand and wait.

10. M: I just heard the most incredible news.
    W: Well, tell me. Don't leave me in the dark.
    What does the woman mean?

    a. She doesn't want the news kept from her.
    b. She wants the man to turn the lights on.
    c. She's afraid to be left alone.
    d. She doesn't want to hear the news.

11. W: Is this computer program similar to the one you've been using?
    M: No, it's a whole new ballgame.
    What does the man mean?

    a. The programs are alike.
    b. The programs are computer games.
    c. The programs are very different.
    d. The programs are new.

12. W: I've got a great idea for our class reunion.
    M: I knew you'd come up with something.
    What does the man mean?

    a. He knew she would bring him something.
    b. He wasn't expecting her to have a plan.
    c. He thought she would be coming to see him.
    d. He was sure she would think up an idea.

13. M: We're looking for someone to go fishing with us on Saturday.
    W: Well, you can count me out.
    What does the woman's comment mean?

    a. She's making plans to go with them.
    b. She doesn't want to go.
    c. She knows how to count.
    d. She wants to stay outside.

14. W: Aren't you fed up with your noisy roommate?
    M: Not really, I've been wearing earplugs!
    What is the woman asking?

    a. If he likes his roommate.
    b. If he has asked his roommate to dinner.
    c. If he is losing patience with his roommate.
    d. If he has any problems with his roommate.

15. M: Are you enjoying your stay here on the islands?
    W: Oh yes. It's a far cry from winter in the Midwest.
    What does the woman mean?

    a. The islands are very different from the Midwest.
    b. The islands are a great distance from the Midwest.
    c. The islands are similar to the Midwest.
    d. The islands make her cry for the Midwest.

B. Confusing Words

There are a number of words in English that often cause problems because they have a similar meaning, or sound alike. In the Structure and Written Expression section of the TOEFL® test, words of a similar meaning or related form are used in error.

One of the most common of these errors involves the verbs **make** and **do.**

MAKE and DO

Many languages have only one verb for **do** and **make.** In English the verb *to do* basically means "to perform, to act," while the verb *to make* means "to produce by action." These two verbs are also found in a number of fixed expressions.

Expressions with MAKE.

make a mistake	make a plan
make war	make an investment
make a comparison	make an offer
make a discovery	make a choice
make use of	make an attempt
make a profit	make a decision
make a suggestion	make a forecast

Expressions with DO

do one's duty	do harm
do homework	do research
do justice to	do an assignment
do business	do one's best
do work	do a service
do wrong	do damage
do a kindness	do wonders

EXERCISE 1

A.   Some of these words can be used with *make* and some with *do,* and some with neither one. Circle the correct answer.

1. a journey	a. do	b. make	c. neither
2. a favor	a. do	b. make	c. neither
3. a service	a. do	b. make	c. neither
4. a fortune	a. do	b. make	c. neither
5. pretend	a. do	b. make	c. neither
6. good	a. do	b. make	c. neither
7. money	a. do	b. make	c. neither
8. a choice	a. do	b. make	c. neither
9. trouble	a. do	b. make	c. neither
10. sure	a. do	b. make	c. neither
11. enemies	a. do	b. make	c. neither
12. the mind	a. do	b. make	c. neither
13. complaint	a. do	b. make	c. neither
14. nothing	a. do	b. make	c. neither
15. friends	a. do	b. make	c. neither
16. progress	a. do	b. make	c. neither
17. use of something	a. do	b. make	c. neither
18. a conclusion	a. do	b. make	c. neither
19. an improvement	a. do	b. make	c. neither
20. wrong	a. do	b. make	c. neither

B.   Now add ten other words that can be used with MAKE.

EXERCISE 2

Put the words in the box under the correct column.

her best	a difference	plans
her duty	a distinction	room
research	a contribution	an improvement
a report	amends	without
a job	way	an examination
a prediction	an escape	a confession

	She Made				She Did		
1. _____	1. _____			1. _____	1. _____		
2. _____	2. _____			2. _____	2. _____		
3. _____	3. _____			3. _____	3. _____		
4. _____	4. _____			4. _____	4. _____		
5. _____	5. _____			5. _____	5. _____		
6. _____	6. _____			6. _____	6. _____		

 EXERCISE 3

Choose the correct word to complete each sentence.

1. Albert Einstein's theories have (made / done) a great contribution to the development of modern science.

2. Bats can hear and distinguish insects by the number of wing beats per second the insect (makes / does).

3. (Making / doing) cloth with the use of synthetic fibers requires less labor than the use of natural fibers.

4. Nostradamus (made / did) predictions for the year 1999 in the sixteenth century.

5. All possible colors can be (made / done) by mixing three primary colors together in various proportions.

6. Eli Whitney's invention (did / made) much to improve the American cotton industry.

7. Pioneer and Voyager are the names of two kinds of American space probes that have (made / done) important discoveries about the solar system.

8. Richard Hoe's invention of the steam cylinder rotary press in 1846, (made / did) it possible for newspapers to be printed at a faster rate.

9. Many advances have been (made / done) in the field of communication through the use of fiber optics.

LIKE and ALIKE

Another word-choice error that appears in the Structure and Written Expression Section of the TOEFL® test is the incorrect use of **like** or **alike** or in the negative form **unlike** or **not alike.**

Like and **alike** both have the same meaning but are used in different patterns.

Like X, Y...

X, like Y...

X is like Y...

but

  X and Y are alike…

  In the negative form **unlike** and **not alike** also have the same meaning but are used in different patterns.

  Unlike X, Y…

  X, unlike Y…

  X is unlike Y…

but

  X and Y are not alike . . .

EXERCISE 4

Choose the correct word to complete each sentence.

1. (Alike / Like) butterflies, moths can be dull-colored or brightly colored.
2. (Alike / Like) other beans, lima beans are seeds that grow in pods.
3. (Not alike / Unlike) oxygen, which is changed in our bodies into carbon dioxide, nitrogen goes back into the air.
4. (Like / Alike) Yellowstone National Park in Wyoming, Wairakei in New Zealand is famous for its hot-spring systems.
5. The first settlers, (alike / like) the American Indians, planted corn and ate pumpkins and squash.
6. Keratin, found in feathers, and the horny substance found in our nails are (alike / like).
7. (Like / Alike) animals, plants need about the same vitamins for growth and development.
8. (Unlike / Not alike) animal tissues, which are soft and flexible, plants retain their form to a large extent.
9. Neanderthal man was not greatly (alike / unlike) modern man in physical structure.

Other Confusing Words

The following are some other confusing words occurring in the Structure and Written Expression section of the TOEFL® test.

1. AFFECT (v)/EFFECT (n)
    Affect means to influence; *effect* means result.

    The tranquilizer was not affecting the animal.
    The tranquilizer had no effect on the animal.

2. AFTER (prep)/AFTERWARDS (adv)
    After means following in time, later than; *afterwards* means after that.

    I will see you after the test.
    I will see you afterwards.

3. ALMOST (adv)/MOST (adj)
Almost means very nearly; *most* means the greatest part.

> Almost everyone passed the test.
> Most students received a passing grade.

4. AMONG (prep)/BETWEEN (prep)
Among is used for three or more persons or things; *between* is used for two persons or things.

> The work was distributed between Paul and John.
> The work was distributed among the members of the team.

5. AMOUNT (n)/NUMBER (n)
Amount is used with non-count nouns; *number* is used with count nouns.

> A great amount of money was spent on housing.
> A great number of houses were being built.

6. ANOTHER (det)/OTHER (det)
Another means one more. It is used before a singular noun or alone. *Other* means the second of the two. It is used before a plural noun or singular noun when preceded by a determiner.

> She needs another piece of paper.
> We have other ideas about this project.

7. BECAUSE (conj)/BECAUSE OF (prep)
Because introduces an adverb clause and is followed by a subject and verb; *because of* is followed by a noun clause.

> Because it was dark, we could not see.
> Because of the dark, we could not see.

8. BEFORE (adv)/AGO (adv)
Ago means in the past; *before* shows the difference between a distant point and a nearer point in the past.

> We graduated five years ago.
> She had already graduated three years before (eight years ago).

9. DIFFER (v)/DIFFERENT (adj)
Differ and *different* mean not the same. They are both followed by "from."

> These two words differ from each other as parts of speech.
> These two words are not different from each other in meaning.

10. FEWER (adj)/LESS (adj)
Both words mean a small quantity or amount; *fewer* is used with count nouns and *less* with non-count nouns.

> There were fewer birds.
> There was less noise.

11. HARD (adj)/HARDLY (adv)
Hard means difficult; *hardly* means scarcely, barely.

> The reading passages were hard.
> He spoke so fast she could hardly understand.

12. LONELY (adj)/ALONE (adj)
Lonely means feeling unhappy and abandoned; *alone* means without others.

> He had no friends and felt lonely.
> He likes to go to the mountains alone.

13. NEAR (adj)/NEARLY (adv)

Near means not far; *nearly* means almost.

> The city is near the ocean.
>
> We nearly missed the train.

14. OLD (adj)/AGE (n)

Old means advanced in age; *age* means the period of time a person or thing has existed.

> Mozart composed music at a very young age.
>
> Mozart composed music when he was five years old.

15. PERCENT (adv)(n)/PERCENTAGE (n)

Percent means one part in each 100; *percentage* means the proportion as a whole of 100.

> The five oceans of the world cover 71 percent of the world's surface.
>
> The percentage of people dying from the disease is increasing every year.

16. TALL(adj)/HIGH (adj)

Tall means having a bigger than average height; *high* means having a top a long distance from the ground. For people and things that are narrow and high, *tall* is used.

> There is a high wall around the palace.
>
> George Washington was a tall man.
>
> The sequoias are tall trees.

Note: Confusing words like *principal* and *principle, elicit* and *illicit, descent* and *decent* where there is a difference in spelling are not tested on the TOEFL®.

Test on Confusing Words

The following sentences contain confusing words. Some sentences are correct and some are not. Write C for correct sentences and I for the incorrect sentences.

_____ 1. Chickens start to lay eggs when they are 18 weeks age.

_____ 2. Nearly 8 percent of the earth's crust is made of aluminum.

_____ 3. When the original 13 states formed a Union, afterward the American Revolution, each representative wanted to have the new capital in his own state.

_____ 4. Our Milky Way alike other similar galaxies, contains stars of varying size.

_____ 5. The sequoia trees, some of which are more than 3,000 years ago, are among the largest and oldest trees in the world.

_____ 6. The higher education system in the United States allows some unit credits to be transferred between universities.

_____ 7. Until the beginning of the 20th century, the majority of Americans continued to do their living from agriculture.

_____ 8. Not alike humans, gorillas live in largely permanent family groups.

_____ 9. The earth went through an immensely hot phase 4,600 million years ago, when it became a molten mass.

_____ 10. The Galapagos penguin lives on the Galapagos Islands nearly the equator.

_____ 11. Many people do the mistake of thinking that pandas are bears when they are actually related to the American raccoon.

_____ 12. A single-masted sailing boat known as a sloop differs from a ketch, which has two masts.

_____ 13. Fog is the affect of the cooling of warm, moist air.

_____ 14. Most ravens are large, stocky, and entirely black.

_____ 15. Captain James Cook, in three voyages from 1768 to 1779, explored more of the Pacific than any another man before him.

CHAPTER 9

Prefixes

illegal
interact
rebuild

A **prefix** is a form added in front of a word or word root to change its meaning. For example, the prefix *il* means "not," therefore the word "illegal" means "not legal." Learning prefixes will help you work out the meaning of many words you do not know in English, and will consequently help you with all parts of the TOEFL® test.

There are more than 50 prefixes in English, and you will work with most of these in this section. We will start by looking at four of these prefixes (*de-*, *inter-*, *pro-*, *dis-*) and some of the words they create.

Reading Practice

Read the following passage.

The tepee was an excellent home for the nomadic Native Americans. It could be put up or disassembled in minutes. Its multipurpose external poles made it possible to roll up the sides in hot weather or reattach them at the bottom in winter. Sometimes a skirt of buffalo skin was hung around the circumference of the tepee, which provided additional insulation from the cold.

Tepees came in a multitude of sizes, from very small to extremely large. Floors were "carpeted" with buffalo skins and the fur of other animals. They were quite comfortable and sometimes rather luxurious.

When the local resources were depleted and a tribe decided to relocate, the tepees were dismantled. Some of the poles were tied to horses, one pole on each side, each with one end on the ground. A tepee cover was rolled up and tied across the two poles. This very special form of transportation was called a "drag" or *travois*. Many such drags were used to carry the belongings from each tepee—utensils, dried meat, and other items. Some drags even had baskets to carry young children. In this way, entire camps of hundreds of people could proceed quickly across the roughest kind of country.

 EXERCISE 1

Work with a partner, with a group, or alone to answer the following questions.

1. What could be done with a tepee in minutes?

Task

The word "assembled" means "put together." What do you think "*dis*assembled" means? What do you think the prefix *dis-* means? Find another word in the passage with this prefix.

2. The poles of the tepee had many purposes. What is the word used for this?

Task

Name two words beginning with this prefix. What do these words mean? Check your answers in a dictionary.

3. What word tells you that the poles were on the outside?

Task

What is the prefix in this word? Name two other words with this prefix.

4. What could be done with the poles in winter?

Task

What do you think the prefix *re-* means? Find another word in the passage with this prefix. What two other words do you know that begin with this prefix?

---

5. What do you think "the circumference of the tepee" means?

Task

Find two other words beginning with this prefix. You may use a dictionary.

6. Why did a tribe decide to relocate?

Task

What do you think the word "deplete" means? Check your answer in a dictionary. What do you think the prefix *de-* means?

7. What was a "drag" or *travois?*

Task

Find two words with the prefix *trans-*. What do you think the prefix *trans-* means?

8. What could hundreds of people do with these drags?

Task

What do you think "proceed" means? What do you think the prefix *pro-* means?

 EXERCISE 2

Work with a partner, with a group, or alone to complete the words with the correct prefixes. Add the prefixes to the word they belong with. You may use each prefix more than once.

de-	multi-	circum-	pro-
re-	trans-	ex-	

1. When the Lewis and Clark _____pedition realized they couldn't _____turn over the mountains until spring, they built a fort to shelter them for the winter.

2. The Statue of Liberty is perhaps the most _____nowned symbol of America.

3. Sir Francis Drake _____navigated the globe from 1577 to 1580.

4. If a lizard's tail somehow becomes _____tached, it will _____generate a new tail.

5. A telescope is used to _____tect and observe far away objects.

6. Streetcars were a major form of _____portation in the 1900s.

7. During photosynthesis, plants _____duce oxygen.

8. A parrot fish is a _____colored tropical marine fish.

- By doing the exercises in this section you will familiarize yourself with the most common prefixes in English. This will enable you to recognize or guess the meaning of hundreds of words.
- A prefix usually changes the meaning of a word. For example, the prefix *in-* changes the meaning of a word to the opposite. "Capable" means "having the ability of doing or being." "Incapable" means "not having the ability of doing or being."
- Prefixes are often attached to roots of words.

EXAMPLES

re	→	act
inter	→	act
trans	→	act

By knowing the prefix and the root, you can work out the meaning of the word.

A. Words Beginning with *De-*

de- =	**down, reversing, away from**

1. **to degenerate** = to go down to a lower condition or a character with low morals.

   Ex. The argument degenerated into a fight.

2. **to deviate** = to move away from what is normal or required.

   Ex. The politician deviated from the subject because he didn't want to answer the question.

3. **to deplete** = to reduce greatly.

   Ex. Due to the war that was going on, food supplies had been depleted.

4. **to decompose** = to break up after death.

   Ex. When organic products decompose, gases useful for power and heat are produced.

5. **to dehydrate** = to remove all the water from.

   Ex. When milk is dehydrated, it forms a powder.

6. **to deflate** = to let air or gas out. Also to reduce the level of prices.

   Ex. The tire was deflated, so he put more air in it.

7. **to depreciate** = to lessen in value or price.

   Ex. Works of art never depreciate in value.

8. **to detect** = to uncover, to find.

   Ex. Small amounts of aluminum were detected in the drinking water.

EXERCISE 1

Circle T if the sentence is TRUE and F if the sentence is FALSE.

1. To decompose means to rewrite.   T   F
2. To lessen in value or price is to depreciate.   T   F
3. To deflate is to reduce in size by letting out gas.   T   F
4. To degenerate is to be less generous.   T   F
5. To look for and to find is to detect.   T   F
6. To dehydrate is to take away all the water from inside a body or object. T   F
7. To deviate is to feel sick when flying.   T   F
8. To deplete is to reduce in quantity.   T   F

EXERCISE 2

Fill in the blanks with one of the following words. Change the verb form as necessary.

to degenerate	to deviate	to deplete	to decompose
to dehydrate	to deflate	to depreciate	to detect

1. High government spending has _____ the gold reserves.
2. Doctors _____ a small piece of bone in her stomach.
3. Food _____ quickly in a hot room.
4. It is sad to see a great man _____ into a criminal.
5. To _____ from the straight route wastes time.
6. We _____ the air bed in order to store it.
7. The greatest danger in the desert is that you will _____.
8. Every year your car _____ by a large amount.

B. Words Beginning with *Inter-*

inter- =   between, among

1. **intermittent** = (adj) stopping for a time and then continuing.

    Ex.   The fever was not continuous but intermittent.

2. **intermediate** = (adj) in the middle level, between two extremes.

Ex. Since the student was neither a beginner nor advanced in her knowledge, she was put in an intermediate class.

3. **to intervene** = to interrupt something, usually to stop something bad from happening.

   Ex. Just as the two groups started to fight, the police intervened.

4. **to intersperse** = to place here and there.

   Ex. The dry plain was interspersed with a few trees.

5. **to intermingle** = mix together or into.

   Ex. The police intermingled with the crowd to catch the thief.

6. **to interrelate** = connect in a way that makes one depend on the other.

   Ex. Reading and writing skills are interrelated.

7. **to interact** = when one has an effect on the other.

   Ex. The show's success was mainly due to the way the comedians interacted with each other.

8. **to intercept** = to catch before it can escape.

   Ex. The guards intercepted the prisoner as he was climbing out of the window.

 EXERCISE 1

Circle T if the sentence is TRUE and F is the sentence is FALSE.

1.	Something which is intermittent stops and then starts again.	T	F
2.	When things are intermingled, they are mixed together like the ingredients of a cake.	T	F
3.	To be interspersed means to be found here and there.	T	F
4.	If something is intercepted, it is forbidden by law.	T	F
5.	The intermediate level is the lowest level.	T	F
6.	To intervene is to have surgery.	T	F
7.	To interact is to act between two events.	T	F
8.	To interrelate means to be a relative of someone.	T	F

 EXERCISE 2

Fill in the blanks with one of the following words.

intervened	intermittent	intermediate	interrelated
intermingled	interspersed	interact	intercepted

1. The rain was _____ all through the day.

2. The students were divided into three groups: beginning, _____, and advanced.

3. When the patient started to weaken dramatically, the doctors _____.

4. The state police _____ the speeding motorist at a road block.

5. To practice a foreign language it is necessary to _____ with other students or native speakers of the language.

6. In economics, supply and demand are _____.

7. The region was with _____ small villages.

8. The sound of the gunshot _____ with the sound of the fireworks, and therefore could not be heard.

C. Words Beginning with *Pro-*

pro-	=	**before, in favor of, forward**

1. **to promote** = to advance a person in position or help something to succeed.

   Ex. The students who pass the final exam will be promoted to the next level.

2. **to proliferate** = to reproduce and increase in number.

   Ex. Rabbits and other rodents proliferate quickly.

3. **to protrude** = to stick out.

   Ex. The point of the arrow protruded from out of the back of the wounded man.

4. **profound** = (adj) deep; a person with a deep understanding and knowledge. Especially used for respect, fear, or silence.

   Ex. Socrates had a profound knowledge and understanding of life.

5. **to proclaim** = to declare or say in public.

   Ex. When the party spokesman proclaimed victory, the crowd cheered.

6. **proficient** = (adj) very skilled in a particular activity.

   Ex. He is a very proficient administrator.

7. **prominent** = (adj) standing out as more important than others.

   Ex. She is a prominent lawyer in this community.

8. **profuse** = (adj) in abundance or plenty.

   Ex. The yellow mimosas were profuse along the mountain road.

9. **prospective** = (adj) used to describe a person who is going to do something.

   Ex. The prospective buyer of the house wanted to know every detail about it.

EXERCISE 1

Match the word with its definition.

proliferate	protrude	proficient
promote	proclaim	prominent
profuse	profound	prospective

1. deep _____

2. increase
   in numbers _____

3. important _____

4. raise in rank _____

5. project out _____

6. expected _____

7. expert in _____

8. announce
   in public _____

9. plenty _____

 EXERCISE 2

Fill in the blanks with one of the words in this lesson.

1. The manager of the hotel was _____ in his apologies for the lack of rooms.

2. A lot of money had been invested to _____ the new product.

3. The holy man was greeted with _____ respect.

4. Abraham Lincoln is a _____ figure in U.S. history.

5. A special dinner was given to the _____ candidate for the leader of the party.

6. The rain helped to _____ the growth of grass everywhere.

7. When the end of the war was _____, people started to dance in the streets.

8. The man had such a _____ jaw that I could not forget his face.

9. He's not only an excellent statesman but very _____ in sailing.

D. Words Beginning with *Dis-*

dis- = reversal, undo, negate

1. **disparity** = inequality; difference in age, condition, character, kind.

   Ex. There is a great disparity in the salaries offered for the same job between the state and the private sector.

2. **to disintegrate** = to separate and form fragments; to break up.

   Ex. The fabric was so old that it disintegrated when I touched it.

3. **to disorient** = to cause someone to lose his or her sense of direction or time.

    Ex.   When he woke up in the hospital after the accident, he was quite disoriented.

4. **to discard** = to throw away.

    Ex.   We will have to discard these documents because they are out of date.

5. **to dissuade** = to persuade or advise someone not to do something.

    Ex.   He wrote a book dissuading people from wearing animal products.

6. **to dissociate** = to separate from the union of someone or something.

    Ex.   The psychiatric patient could not dissociate the real and the fantasy world he lived in.

7. **to disprove** = to prove false.

    Ex.   The theory that all the planets went around the earth was disproved by Copernicus in 1543.

8. **dissimilar** = (adj) not similar, unlike. It is used generally when the contrast is obvious.

    Ex.   The two sisters are quite dissimilar in both character and appearance.

9. **disinterested** = a person who is not influenced by emotion or personal gain when deciding in favor or against something.

    Ex.   A disinterested judge had to be found to settle the dispute.

 EXERCISE **1**

Circle T if the sentence is TRUE and F if the sentence is FALSE.

1. If you want to stop someone from doing something you can try to dissuade them.   T   F
2. You disprove something you do not like.   T   F
3. If you quit an organization, you might want to dissociate yourself from it completely.   T   F
4. When one bird is bigger than another, there is disparity.   T   F
5. By throwing something in the trash you discard it.   T   F
6. A disinterested person is bored.   T   F
7. When something falls to pieces it disintegrates.   T   F
8. Things that are dissimilar are not alike.   T   F

 EXERCISE **2**

Fill in the blanks with one of the following words. Change the verb form as necessary.

to discard	to dissuade	disparity	disinterested
to dissociate	dissimilar	to disorient	to disintegrate
to disprove			

1. There is a great _____ in living standards between rich and poor countries.

2. To avoid problems, a banker must try to remain _____ when deciding about a loan.

3. Because of the danger, his mother tried to _____ him from parachuting off the Eiffel Tower.

4. Nothing will _____ you faster than trying to drive in a strange new city with no map.

5. Everyone thinks the world is round but I shall _____ it.

6. The organization _____ after the president and all his top managers left.

7. You can easily see which twin is which; their styles are quite _____.

8. Smith is such a troublemaker you had better _____ yourself from his activities quickly.

9. Most people _____ junk mail without even opening it.

E.   Other Prefixes

 EXERCISE 1

Work with a partner or a group. Find two examples for each prefix. Then check your examples in a dictionary.

Prefix	Area of Meaning	Examples
ambi-	both	*ambidextrous, ambiguous*
ante-	before	
anti-	against, opposite	
auto-	self	
bi-	two	
circum-	around	
co-, col-, com-, cor-	around	
counter-	in opposition to	
de-	down, out	
dec-	ten	
demi-	half	
dis-	not, bad	
ex-, e-	out of, from	
extra-	beyond	
hemi-	half	
hyper-	beyond	
il-, im-, in-, ir-	not	
inter-	between	
macro-	large	
mal-	bad, badly	

Prefix	Area of Meaning	Examples
micro-	small	
mini-	little, small	
mis-	wrong	
mono-	one	
multi-	many	
non-	no, not	
ob-	in the way of	
over-	too much	
pan-	all, worldwide	
poly-	many	
post-	after, behind	
pre-	before	
pro-	for, on the side of	
re-	again, back	
semi-	half	
sub-	under	
super-	above, more than	
syn-	with, at the same time	
trans-	across	
tri-	three	
under-	not enough	
ni-	one, single	
un-	no, not	
ultra-	beyond	
vice-	deputy	

 EXERCISE 2

Work with a partner, with a group, or alone.

ir-	il-	im-	in-	un-

Use one of the prefixes above to give the adjective the opposite meaning.

1. an _____polite person

2. an _____relevant question

3. an _____formal dinner

4. an _____legible letter

5. an _____responsible driver

6. an _____curable disease

7. an _____familiar place

8. an _____trustworthy friend

9. an _____popular teacher

10. _____mature behavior

11. an _____expected event

12. an _____impressive paper

13. an _____ literate person

14. an _____ capable performer

15. an _____ significant fact

16. an _____ logical idea

17. an _____ reparable damage

18. an _____ legitimate act

19. an _____ reversible decision

20. an _____ pure liquid solution

 EXERCISE 3

Work with a partner, a group, or alone. Make derivatives or form words by adding *bi-, non-, inter-,* or *semi-,* to the following words:

1. stop
2. final
3. partisan
4. aggression
5. member
6. intervention
7. operative
8. existence
9. cultural
10. official
11. domesticated
12. literate

 EXERCISE 4

Work with a partner, a group, or alone. Make derivatives or form words by adding *post-, pre-, anti-,* or *counter-,* to the following words:

1. productive
2. act
3. attack
4. arrange
5. body
6. war
7. colonial
8. semitic
9. social
10. climax
11. toxic
12. historic

Test on Prefixes

Choose the answer that could best replace the underlined word without changing the meaning of the sentence.

1. Ultrasonic waves can <u>detect</u> cracks in metal that the human eye cannot see.

    (A) stop   (B) find   (C) arrange   (D) mend

2. The <u>profuse</u> tropical forests of the Amazon are inhabited by different kinds of animals.

    (A) wild   (B) distant   (C) abundant   (D) immersed

3. When high fever is present, <u>disorientation</u> may occur.

    (A) disposition   (B) confusion   (C) complication   (D) depression

4. The sawfish is easily recognized by its <u>prominent</u> sawlike head.

    (A) protruding   (B) promiscuous   (C) rugged   (D) spiked

5. A government's economic resources must not be <u>depleted</u>.

    (A) wasted   (B) greatly reduced   (C) badly destroyed   (D) disorganized

6. In the seventeenth century, German astronomer Johannes Kepler <u>disproved</u> Pythagoras' theory that the earth was the center of the universe.

    (A) praised   (B) confirmed   (C) misrepresented   (D) denied

7. When sea creatures died millions of years ago, their remains <u>decomposed</u> and were changed into oil and gas.

    (A) broke up   (B) dispersed   (C) detached   (D) combined

8. James McNeil Whistler <u>promoted</u> the idea of art for art's sake.

    (A) put forward   (B) disproved   (C) fought   (D) acquired

9. A giant fungus possessing a <u>uniform</u> genetic composition covering 1,500 acres was found in Washington state.

    (A) unified   (B) straight   (C) covered   (D) single

10. Although Langston Hughes is better known for his poetry, he also wrote a two-volume <u>autobiography</u>.

    (A) book about someone else's life   (B) book about his own life

    (C) book about many people's lives   (D) book about the life of animals

11. Bacteria reproduce most commonly through <u>binary</u> fission (splitting).

    (A) single   (B) multiple   (C) double   (D) triple

12. Samuel Becket is known for his plays about the overwhelming desire to communicate in the face of human <u>disintegration</u>.

    (A) breakdown   (B) division   (C) survival   (D) disparity

CHAPTER 10

Theme Grouping: Places and Movement

Another way of building your vocabulary is by looking at words with similar meanings in themes. For example, if we take the theme "Moving and Not Moving," we find there are several words that mean "not moving" but each is slightly different in its meaning and use. The word "inert" means "not moving" and is used for things that do not have the power to act or move, whereas the word "stagnant" is used mainly for water that is not moving.

In this section there are different themes with exercises that accompany them. Since only a certain number of themes can be covered in this book, it is suggested that you start to make your own themes with the use of a dictionary in order to continue to build your vocabulary.

Reading Practice

Read the following passage.

Many animals mimic leaves. The most successful are insects, whose veined wings are ideally suited to change into leaf-like shapes and surfaces, but there are also excellent vertebrate examples among chameleons, toads, frogs, and fish. All sorts of leaves are used as models—fresh green leaves, dead brown leaves, rotting leaves, and even falling leaves.

The most remarkable leaf mimic among the vertebrates are the South American leaf fish from the Amazon valley, and the bat fish from Indo-Pacific coasts. The leaf fish is a generalized leaf mimic which lives in freshwater streams. On the other hand, the bat fish specifically resembles mangrove leaves and lives in the shallow water in which mangroves grow. The construction of the leaf fish resembles that of a horizontal leaf, and the bat fish looks like a vertical leaf. The leaf fish is a predator of other fish and makes use of its disguise to stalk prey. It floats on its side, like a leaf, just below the surface of the water, and propels itself along with no apparent movement using its fins. In this way, looking like a drifting leaf, it creeps upon unsuspecting fish, until with a final thrust it engulfs its prey. On the other hand, the disguise of the bat fish seems mainly protective.

It floats gently along, moving only its transparent tail, sometimes twisting and swaying in exactly the manner of drifting mangrove leaves. When danger threatens, it goes down and stays inert at the sea bottom where it lies stationary among the leaves it so much resembles.

 EXERCISE 1

Work with a partner, with a group, or alone to answer the following questions.

1. How does the leaf fish move?

Task

Name two things that "propel."

2. How does the leaf fish engulf its prey?

Task

What two other things can you "thrust"?

3. How does the bat fish stay when it is at the bottom of the sea?

Task

What other word in the passage means "with no movement"? Give an example using each of these words which mean "no movement."

Conversation Practice

Read the following conversation.

Susan:	Hi, Joshua. Are you coming down to the beach today to play volleyball?
Joshua:	I'd love to, but I promised my parents I would do some yardwork today.
Susan:	If I helped you, would you be able to go? You're our most **dynamic** player. We need you on our team.
Joshua:	Sure. If we work together, we should be done in about two hours.
Susan:	Great! We'll be just in time for the game. Where do I start?
Joshua:	Take this trimmer and trim the **border** around this walkway. Be careful because that tool has a very sharp **edge.**
Susan:	What are you going to do?
Joshua:	I'll trim the hedges at the **boundary** of our property. It's best that I do that job because my mother likes them trimmed a certain way and there isn't much **margin** for error.
Susan:	OK, I'll get started here. By the way, do you want me to take this **stagnant** water out of the bird bath?
Joshua:	Yes, I suppose it should be **drawn** out of there.
Susan:	Why don't we just **heave** it on its side?
Joshua:	Because the tiny stones at the bottom will **scatter** everywhere.
Susan:	I see. In that case, I'll just use this little scoop to **extract** the water.
Joshua:	Great idea. I'll **drag** the hose over here so you can refill the bath with fresh water.
Susan:	I'll take care of that. Now, you'd better **shift** over to your job or we'll never get to the game today.
Joshua:	We'll see how much you feel like playing after you've been bending over that walkway for an hour.
Susan:	Don't worry about me. I'm as **agile** as a cat. I'll get through this in no time.
Joshua:	In that case, let's get started.

 EXERCISE 2

Work with a partner, with a group, or alone to answer the following questions.

1. Why does Susan need Joshua on her team?

Task

Give an example of a person with this characteristic.

2. What does Joshua want Susan to clip with the trimmer?

Task

Find another word that is similar to "border" in the conversation.

3. Why must Susan be careful of the tool?

Task

Name two things with a sharp edge.

4. Why must Joshua trim the hedges?

Task

What do you think "margin for error" means?

5. What kind of water is there in the bird bath?

Task

What kind of water do you think this is? What is the word "stagnant" usually associated with?

6. What does Joshua suggest be done with the water?

Task

What do you think "draw out" means? What things can you draw out?

7. What does Susan suggest be done with the bird bath?

Task

What do you think heave means? Name two things you "heave."

8. If they heave the bird bath on its side, what will happen to the stones at the bottom?

Task

What do you think "scatter" means? Name two things that can be "scattered."

A. Boundaries and Borders

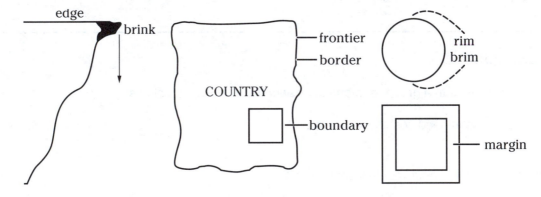

1. **border** = the place where one country touches another.

    Ex. The guards at the border stopped all the cars.

2. **frontier** = the place where one country touches another, or the border of something known and unknown. It is also used in U.S. history to mean the border between settled and wild country.

    Ex. In 1840 the settlers crossed the frontier to the west in their wagons.

3. **boundary** = the limit or edge of a place (not a country), e.g., a piece of land.

    Ex. The house was built right on the boundary of the city.

4. **edge** = the end of something high, or the thinnest part of something that can cut.

    Ex. My new knife has a really sharp edge.

5. **brink** = the edge of something dangerous or high.

    Ex. The situation is very tense, and the country is on the brink of war.

6. **rim** = the outside edge of something round, e.g., glasses, cups, eye-glasses, wheels.

    Ex. He filled the glass right up to the rim.

7. **brim** = the outside edge of a hat used for protection against the sun or rain, or the outside edge of a cup or bowl.

    Ex. The sombrero is a hat with a wide brim.

8. **margin** = the spaces left on the top, bottom, and sides of a piece of paper. It is also used for an amount over what is necessary.

    Ex. You have a ten-day margin to complete the work.

9. **limit** = the farthest point you can go.

    Ex. With his talent there is no limit to where he can go.

EXERCISE 1

One word in each group does not belong. Find the word.

1. frontier boundary border rim
2. brim rim brink
3. edge brink rim
4. margin rim brim
5. brink rim limit

EXERCISE 2

Choose the correct word to complete each sentence.

1. The (brim / rim) of a cowboy's hat protects him from the sun.
2. Don't forget to leave a narrower (border / margin) on the left-hand side of your sheet of paper.
3. The speed (limit / margin) is 55 m.p.h. and you are driving at 70 m.p.h.
4. The (boundary / limit) of the field is marked by a white line.
5. The 1980s were the (frontier / brink) of the computer age.
6. He was on the (brink / edge) of death when the ambulance arrived.
7. She bought a new pair of sunglasses with silver (rims / edges).
8. He was just standing on the (edge / brink) of the swimming pool.
9. After peace talks between the two countries, the guards along the (border / limit) were reduced.

B. Moving and Not Moving

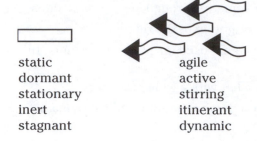

static	agile
dormant	active
stationary	stirring
inert	itinerant
stagnant	dynamic

1. **agile** = quick moving; often used for sports or action to get out of trouble.

    Ex.   Both wild and domestic cats are agile.

2. **active** = moving about, doing things.

    Ex.   Although he has retired, he is still very active in politics.

3. **itinerant** = traveling from place to place, usually to practice a profession or work at a job.

    Ex.   In the past itinerant judges went from town to town in the West.

4. **dynamic** = producing power and activity; an energetic person.

    Ex.   He was so dynamic raising money for the homeless, he collected six million dollars.

5. **stirring** = that which excites feelings.

    Ex.   The leader gave a stirring speech.

6. **static** = not moving or changing.

    Ex.   The situation was static with the two armies facing each other.

7. **stationary** = staying in one place, not moving.

    Ex.   For the last week rates of interest have remained stationary.

8. **stagnant** = water that is not moving or flowing, usually with a bad smell.

    Ex.   Many insects like pools of stagnant water.

9. **inert** = not having the power to move or act.

    Ex.   Some comets are made up of inert matter.

10. **dormant** = not active temporarily, as if asleep.

    Ex.   The volcano erupted after having been dormant for 120 years.

EXERCISE 1

Circle T if the sentence is TRUE and F if the sentence is FALSE.

1. Something stirring can make you excited.	T	F
2. Stagnant water moves fast.	T	F
3. Agile means someone who is growing old.	T	F
4. Someone dynamic is full of energy.	T	F

5. Active people do not like doing things.   T   F
6. Something dormant appears to be asleep.   T   F
7. Static means not moving or changing.   T   F
8. An itinerant person goes from place to place.   T   F

 EXERCISE 2

Complete the sentences with the correct answer.

1. _____ workers follow the crops from town to town.
   a. Static   b. Dynamic   c. Itinerant

2. If there are mosquitoes in your home there is _____ water nearby.
   a. stagnant   b. static   c. dormant

3. Basketball players need to be fit and _____.
   a. stirring   b. agile   c. inert

4. When we saw the _____ body of the dog in our yard we knew there was trouble.
   a. itinerant   b. agile   c. inert

5. As long as the high pressure remains _____ over our area the weather will be hot,
   hot, hot!
   a. static   b. agile   c. stagnant

6. One thousand people singing together is a _____ experience.
   a. dormant   b. dynamic   c. stirring

7. His body may be sick but his brain is still _____.
   a. dormant   b. stirring   c. active

8. My eighty-year-old uncle is so _____ he makes everyone else tired.
   a. dynamic   b. itinerant   c. inert

9. The price of housing has remained _____ for six months.
   a. agile   b. dynamic   c. stationary

10. After the factory closed the machinery lay _____.
    a. stirring   b. dormant   c. active

C. Pushing and Pulling

thrust
project
propel
scatter
eject

shift
drag
draw
heave
extract

1. **to shift** = to move from one place to another or from one direction to another.

   Ex.   The wind shifted direction during the night to a northerly direction.

2. **to drag** = to pull something along the ground.

   Ex.   The ant dragged the leaf across the ground.

3. **to draw** = to take or pull out over a period of time.

   Ex.   In ancient times, blood was drawn as a cure for many illnesses.

4. **to heave** = to lift something heavy with great effort.

   Ex.   The sailors heaved the huge shark over the side.

5. **to extract** = to take out physically or with an instrument or by chemical means.

   Ex.   Oil is extracted from peanuts.

6. **to thrust** = to push with force.

   Ex.   Forces in the earth's crust thrust land masses together causing mountains to rise.

7. **to project** = to stand out forward from something.

   Ex.   Ridges of rock projected out along the coastline.

8. **to propel** = to move, drive, or push forward.

   Ex.   The wind propels the sails of a windmill.

9. **to scatter** = to throw here and there with no plan.

   Ex.   The wind scatters the seeds of many trees.

10. **to eject** = to throw out by force, usually from within.

    Ex.   The volcano ejected lava over a surface of several square miles.

 EXERCISE **1**

Circle T if the sentence is TRUE and F if the sentence is FALSE.

1.	To propel is to move, drive or push forward.	T	F
2.	To project is to keep from harm.	T	F
3.	To thrust is to believe in pushing.	T	F
4.	To throw everywhere with no plan is to scatter.	T	F
5.	To draw out is to take out over a period of time.	T	F
6.	To eject is to throw out with force.	T	F
7.	To drag is to pull along the ground.	T	F
8.	To extract is to take out by mechanical, physical, or chemical means.	T	F

EXERCISE 2

Complete the sentences with the correct answer.

1. The sergeant _____ his head round the door and shouted at us to get out of bed.

   a. ejected   b. dragged   c. thrust

2. It is difficult to argue with him because he always _____ his point of view.

   a. shifts   b. heaves   c. extracts

3. Magnificent horns _____ from the stag's head.

   a. scattered   b. projected   c. propelled

4. Some dentists _____ teeth less painfully than others.

   a. extract   b. scatter   c. heave

5. Quick as lightning he _____ the snake out the door.

   a. drew   b. dragged   c. propelled

6. When he switched on the fan, papers _____ everywhere.

   a. projected   b. scattered   c. thrust

7. The crazy scientist tried to _____ sunlight from fruit.

   a. shift   b. drag   c. extract

8. The guard _____ the noisy protestor from the hall.

   a. projected   b. ejected   c. scattered

9. Slowly she _____ the heavy suitcase upstairs.

   a. thrust   b. propelled   c. dragged

10. The bank guard _____ the bag of gold into the truck.

    a. heaved   b. shifted   c. extracted

Test on Places and Movement

1. Nitrogen is largely <u>an inert</u> gas and liquefies easily.

   (A) a prevalent   (B) a motionless   (C) a stagnant   (D) a unique

2. In 1861, the North and South were on the <u>brink</u> of war.

   (A) rim   (B) margin   (C) ege   (D) frontier

3. Licorice is <u>extracted</u> from the liquorice plant which belongs to the family of beans.

   (A) dragged from   (B) projected from   (C) taken from   (D) ejected from

4. After being <u>dormant</u> for 129 years, Mount St. Helens erupted.

   (A) inactive   (B) inert   (C) stagnant   (D) static

5. Leeches were once commonly used to <u>draw</u> blood.

   (A) drag   (B) eject   (C) heave   (D) extract

6. The seeds of the maple are <u>scattered</u> by the wind.

   (A) stirred   (B) itinerant   (C) dispersed   (D) dragged

7. Penguins are not very <u>agile</u>.

   (A) itinerant   (B) active   (C) stationary   (D) stirring

8. In his <u>stirring</u> speech "I Have a Dream," Martin Luther King described the future of racial harmony.

   (A) moving   (B) active   (C) agile   (D) static

9. Squid use the force of their ten long arms to <u>propel</u> themselves through the water.

   (A) scatter   (B) push   (C) catch   (D) drag

10. <u>Stagnant</u> water around a home should always be removed, as it is a breeding place for mosquitos.

    (A) Moving   (B) Swirling   (C) Still   (D) Muddy

11. The small Cupeno native tribe flourished from pre-Colombian times to 1903 and lived in the mountains <u>bordering</u> today's San Diego County.

    (A) touching the edge of   (B) at some distance from

    (C) within the limits of   (D) in the middle of

12. During hibernation, animals remain <u>dormant</u> and their heart rate, breathing, and temperature are very low.

    (A) awake   (B) agile   (C) comfortable   (D) motionless

CHAPTER **11**

Theme Grouping: Size

Reading Practice

Read the following passage.

Because of their **diminutive** size and brilliant colors, hummingbirds stand out as among nature's most remarkable creatures. There are more than 300 kinds of hummingbirds, with the greatest number inhabiting Central and South America.

Their feathers have no solid color. Instead, each feather has **miniscule** barbs, placed so they reflect light, just like a diamond. The hummingbird's whirring wing-beats are made possible by special hinges within their bone structure that allow helicopter-like rapid vibrating. **Prolonged** suspended and backward flight require about 54 wing-beats per second. Because it uses so much energy in flight, a hummingbird goes into a **diminished** state of energy resembling hibernation at night when it rests from the constant work of gathering food.

The female hummingbird is responsible for building its **miniature**, yet solid nest. It then takes 21 days for her pea-sized eggs to hatch. For three weeks she will perform the duty of feeding her hungry chicks, when finally they are ready to fly and to join the rest of their remarkable bird family.

EXERCISE 1

Work with a partner, with a group, or alone to answer the following questions.

1. What is special about hummingbirds?

Task

What do you think "diminutive" means? Name one thing that is diminutive.

2. What do hummingbirds have on each feather?

Task

What do you think "miniscule" means? Name two things that are miniscule.

3. What kinds of flight require 54 wing-beats per second?

Task

What do you think "prolonged" means? What other things can you prolong?

4. What happens to the hummingbird at night because it uses so much energy?

Task

What do you think "diminished" means? Give two other verbs with a similar meaning.

5. What kind of nest does the female hummingbird build?

Task

What kinds of miniature things have you seen or know about?

Conversation Practice

Read the following conversation.

Margaret:	Hi! I tried to call you yesterday. Where were you?
Jeremy:	I went to the Natural History Museum to see their **expanded** dinosaur exhibit.
Margaret:	Did you like it?
Jeremy:	Oh, yes. It's amazing to see how big most of the dinosaurs were. The full-sized models **dwarf** everything else at the museum.
Margaret:	I'll have to go see it for myself. Maybe I'll get some information for my biology term paper. I want to write about the theories concerning the **decline** and extinction of the dinosaurs.
Jeremy:	Well, there's lots of information at the museum that could **augment** your library research.
Margaret:	Good, then I'll definitely go on Saturday.
Jeremy:	Let me know how you like it.
Margaret:	I will. See you after class!
Jeremy:	OK. Bye!

 EXERCISE 2

Work with a partner, with a group, or alone to answer the following questions.

1. What did Jeremy go to see at the Natural History Museum?

Task

What does he mean by an "expanded" exhibit? Why would the exhibit be expanded?

2. What do the full-size dinosaur models do in relation to things at the museum?

Task

What do you think "dwarf" means? Why do people grow dwarf fruit trees and other plants?

3. What does Margaret want to write about for her biology paper?

Task

What do you think "decline" means? Name something that has declined in recent years.

4. How could the information at the museum help Margaret with her biology term paper?

Task

What do you think "augment" means? How can you augment your vocabulary?

A. Size: Small

tiny	minute	diminutive	dwarf
minuscule	minimal	miniature	microscopic

1. **tiny** = very small.

    Ex.   A newly-born baby has tiny hands and feet.

2. **minute** = very small

    Ex.   All the information you need is stored in a minute chip in the computer.

3. **diminutive** = very small and less heavily built.

    Ex.   As technology has progressed, more diminutive versions of the pocket calculator may be seen such as on watches.

4. **dwarf** = like a person, animal, or plant that is below the normal size of its kind, which may look deformed.

    Ex.   Dwarf fruit trees usually bear normal size fruit.

5. **minuscule** = very, very small.

    Ex.   The minuscule print was difficult to read.

6. **minimal** = of the smallest possible amount or degree.

    Ex.   The injuries he suffered from the accident were only minimal.

7. **miniature** = a very small copy or example of something.

    Ex.   Miniature portraits the size of a coin were popular at one time.

8. **microscopic** = so small it can only be seen with special equipment.

    Ex.   Though microscopic in size, the flu virus can have fatal effects on old people.

EXERCISE 1

Circle T if the sentence is TRUE and F if the sentence is FALSE.

1. Minute means so brief it takes only sixty seconds.   T   F
2. Something minimal comes in small sizes.   T   F
3. Tiny means very small.   T   F
4. Something dwarf is smaller than others of its kind.   T   F
5. Diminutive means small and lighter in weight.   T   F
6. Something minuscule is very, very light in weight.   T   F
7. Microscopic things cannot be seen with your eyes.   T   F
8. Something miniature is a copy smaller than natural size.   T   F

EXERCISE 2

Complete the sentences with the correct answer.

1. _____ beans are sweeter and tastier than big ones.

   a. Dwarf b. Microscopic c. Minimal

2. The _____ doberman is still a good guard dog.

   a. minuscule b. minute c. miniature

3. The detectives took the dead man's clothes for a _____ examination.

   a. microscopic b. miniature c. tiny

4. For a big man he has _____ feet and even smaller ears.

   a. minimal b. dwarf c. tiny

5. With a _____ effort he won a million dollars.

   a. minimal b. diminutive c. microscopic

6. She may be a _____ old lady but she still races cars.

   a. dwarf b. minuscule c. diminutive

7. The restaurant was expensive and the steaks were _____.

   a. microscopic b. dwarf c. minuscule

8. We were surprised that such a _____ piece of glass could let the air out of the tire.

   a. minute b. diminutive c. minimal

B. Growing and Getting Bigger

expand	swamp	prosper	prolong
amplify	boom	flourish	
augment	boost	swell	

1. **to expand** = (by/into) to grow larger. (This is the most general term meaning to grow bigger.)

   Ex. A dry sponge expands when soaked in water.

2. **to amplify** = to make larger or increase the strength of something. It is especially used for the increase of sound.

   Ex. There are several kinds of devices that can be used to amplify a speaker's voice.

3. **to augment** = to make bigger; to grow more than before.

   Ex. The new victory augmented his confidence even more.

143

4. **to swamp** = (used in the passive) to have too much of something.

    Ex. We are swamped with work and have been working overtime all week.

5. **to boom** = to grow rapidly or increase in value.

    Ex. The housing market was booming last year.

6. **to boost** = to lift up or make grow with some help.

    Ex. Free samples were given with every purchase to boost sales of the new product.

7. **to prosper** = to continue to succeed in life, health, and wealth.

    Ex. There was no other store like it in the village and its business prospered.

8. **to flourish** = to grow with strength and expand.

    Ex. The plants in the garden flourished under her care.

9. **to swell** = to expand from the normal size of something.

    Ex. When he broke his finger, it started to swell.

10. **to prolong** = to make longer in time.

    Ex. He prolonged his stay by an extra two days.

 EXERCISE **1**

Circle T if the sentence is TRUE and F if the sentence is FALSE.

1.	To boom is to grow fast and gain in worth.	T	F
2.	To be swamped is to need more of something.	T	F
3.	To boost is to kick hard.	T	F
4.	To be successful and continue that way is to prosper	T	F
5.	To augment is to grow after a noisy argument.	T	F
6.	To grow with strength and expand is to flourish.	T	F
7.	To improve the strength of something is to amplify.	T	F
8.	To make longer in time is to prolong.	T	F

 EXERCISE **2**

Complete the sentences with one of the following words. Change the verb form as necessary.

expand	amplify	augment	swamp
boom	boost	prosper	flourish
swell	prolong		

1. He _____ his argument with many examples.

2. Thanks to hard work and a lot of luck his company _____.

3. It was so nice by the ocean that they _____ their stay.

4. With love and a healthy diet, the children _____.

5. The star player was _____ by his teammates.

6. When he breathes in, his chest _____ by six inches.

7. The latest victory _____ their chances of winning the series.

8. California has _____ over the last decade.

9. Running _____ your pulse rate.

10. The rotten fruit _____ until it burst.

C. Getting Smaller

1. **to shrink** = to become smaller in size.

   Ex. Wool often shrinks when it is washed in hot water.

2. **to decline** = to fall after a higher or the highest point has been achieved in power, achievement, or wealth.

   Ex. His power began to decline after he lost a succession of battles and territories.

3. **to diminish** = become smaller. It is often used to show how much is lost by something.

   Ex. After raising taxes, the government's popularity started to diminish.

4. **to condense** = to reduce something without losing much of its contents.

   Ex. The four-page article was condensed into a paragraph.

5. **to contract** = to become smaller, usually by a force within.

   Ex. By contracting and dilating, the heart circulates blood around the body.

6. **to subside** = to become less; to go back to normal; to fall.

   Ex. Before starting on their journey, they waited for the strong winds to subside.

7. **to abate** = to reduce something which is excessive in amount such as wind, storms, and pain.

   Ex. The strong pain in his stomach showed no sign of abating.

8. **to decrease** = to become less in number, strength, or quality.

   Ex. When mixed with more water, the strength of the solution will decrease.

9. **to reduce** = to make something smaller or cheaper or to bring it down.

   Ex. If we want to be competitive we have to reduce the price of our goods.

10. **to dwindle** = to become less little by little.

    Ex. The figure moved away and gradually dwindled into a point on the horizon.

EXERCISE 1

Circle T if the sentence is TRUE and F if the sentence is FALSE.

1. When something strong becomes weaker it abates.   T   F
2. To reduce is to make something less valuable.   T   F

3. If something falls back to where it was, it subsides.   T   F
4. To condense is to make smaller without losing content.   T   F
5. If you decrease something you make it flatter.   T   F
6. Something which declines falls from its high point.   T   F
7. To diminish is to become smaller, often in quality.   T   F
8. To dwindle is to become less little by little.   T   F

EXERCISE 2

Complete the sentence with the correct answer.

1. After five hours the storm _____.

   a. contracted   b. abated   c. shrank

2. In bright light the pupils of your eyes _____.

   a. contract   b. diminish   c. dwindle

3. Ten minutes after winning the lottery his joy _____.

   a. subsided   b. condensed   c. reduced

4. Hikers can buy _____ milk which is easier to carry.

   a. abated   b. dwindled   c. condensed

5. After changing their product, sales _____.

   a. diminished   b. condensed   c. abated

6. The number of cigarette smokers has _____ in the United States.

   a. subsided   b. condensed   c. decreased

7. Meat _____ when you cook it.

   a. dwindles   b. abates   c. shrinks

8. We _____ our water bill by washing the car once a week.

   a. reduced   b. subsided   c. condensed

9. The planet's resources _____ as the years go by.

   a. condense   b. abate   c. dwindle

10. Natural diasters can cause the greatest nations to _____.

    a. decrease   b. decline   c. reduce

Test on Size

Choose the answer that could best replace the underlined word without changing the meaning of the sentence.

1. Miniatures became very popular during the 16th and 17th centuries.
   - (A) Small plants
   - (B) Short stories
   - (C) Small pictures
   - (D) Short compositions

2. A lie detector detects minute changes in the temperature of a person's skin.
   - (A) dormant
   - (B) momentary
   - (C) dwarf
   - (D) tiny

3. The plant life in tundra regions include mosses, dwarf shrubs, and some flowers.
   - (A) microscopic
   - (B) minuscule
   - (C) minimal
   - (D) diminutive

4. The jute, a relative of the basswood trees, flourishes in warm, humid climates.
   - (A) amplifies
   - (B) swells
   - (C) thrives
   - (D) prolongs

5. Originally developed for Southern California, the Richter Scale was expanded for worldwide use.
   - (A) prolonged
   - (B) enlarged
   - (C) minuscule
   - (D) swamped

6. The transatlantic telegraph cable is broken by a number of relay stations to boost the signal.
   - (A) strengthen
   - (B) prosper
   - (C) swell
   - (D) subside

7. Viruses are microscopic organisms that cause a number of important diseases in man, animals and even plants.
   - (A) extremely minute
   - (B) very active
   - (C) out of proportion
   - (D) enlarged

8. Many California mining towns prospered until the gold ran out and prospectors moved on to new areas, leaving boom towns to become ghost towns.
   - (A) declined
   - (B) assembled
   - (C) employed
   - (D) thrived

9. Excessive amounts of lead in the air can decrease a child's intelligence.
   - (A) boom
   - (B) diminish
   - (C) abate
   - (D) swamp

10. Supplies of natural gas are diminishing.
    - (A) dwindling
    - (B) contracting
    - (C) swelling
    - (D) condensing

CHAPTER 12

Suffixes

CONFIDE
CONFID**ENCE**
CONFID**ENTIALITY**

A **suffix** is a combination of letters added to the end of a word, or word root. Suffixes are used either to form new words or show the function of a word. For example, the suffix *-ist* or *-ian* added to a noun describes people, forming words like "motor**ist**" and "musi**cian**."

In the TOEFL®, errors in suffixes or word forms are frequently tested in the Structure and Written Expression section where *one* part of speech is used in place of another. For example, the word *dense* will be used instead of *densely*.

In this chapter you will learn some common suffixes that identify nouns, verbs, adjectives, and adverbs to help you recognize errors in word forms. You can also improve your vocabulary as you learn how these common suffixes change words from one part of speech to another.

Reading Practice

Read the following passage.

Sally Ride became the first American woman astronaut in June 1983. She was accepted into the space program in 1978. For five years, Sally went through the difficult training course that prepared her to go into space on the shuttle Challenger. Completing the lengthy and demanding program and the space mission took fearlessness, dedication, and endurance. According to Sally, all the work was worthwhile the moment the space shuttle took off. Sally, a mission specialist, was joined by four other astronauts including mission commander Robert Crippen, pilot Frederick Hauck, mission specialist John Fabian, and the spacecraft's doctor Norman Thagard. The mission lasted 146 hours and did more than any earlier shuttle mission. It put two satellites into space, ran several experiments, and used a robot arm to launch and retrieve a satellite. Sally played an important role when she helped to release the two communications satellites and ran several experiments. It was a successful and historic mission. The experiments went very well, the crew avoided space sickness, and Sally Ride proved that women have an important place in America's space program.

 EXERCISE **1**

Work with a partner, with a group, or alone to answer these questions.

1. Write *three* words that show the qualities Sally had to have in order to complete the program and space mission.

_____   _____   _____

Task

Find one other word for each ending. Look in a dictionary. Are these words nouns or adjectives?

2. What was Sally's job on the space mission?

Task

Name three other jobs with this ending. Look in a dictionary. Are these words nouns or adjectives?

3. What was Robert Crippen's job?

Task

Name three other jobs with this ending. Look in a dictionary. Are these words nouns or adjectives?

4. What two words in the passage describe the mission?

_____   _____

Task

Look in a dictionary. Are these words nouns, adjectives, or adverbs?

Which of the two endings above can be added to the following words?

1. event _____
2. athlete _____
3. artist _____
4. faith _____
5. power _____
6. rhythm _____

EXERCISE 2

Work with a partner, with a group, or alone to add the correct endings to the underlined words.

-ness,	–ic,	–ful,	–ation,	–ence,	–er,	–ist

1. Henry David Thoreau was a <u>write_____</u> and a <u>natural_____</u>.

2. A hologram of an object is made on a piece of <u>photograph_____</u> film by using a laser.

3. Many coral reef fishes have bright colors warning predators that they are <u>distaste_____</u>.

4. All bread that is made to rise depends on a process called <u>ferment_____</u>.

5. After the tadpole develops legs and lungs, we see the <u>emerge_____</u> of an adult frog.

6. Genghis Khan, known for his <u>fierce_____</u>, captured Beijing, most of Persia, and Russian Turkestan in the 1200s.

STRATEGIES

- You do not have to know the meaning of the word to recognize what part of speech it is. You can recognize the characteristic forms of each word. The following example is a nonsense sentence:

    Togonapism fotted osiropation leposly.

    Although we do not know the meaning of these words, we can recognize characteristic forms such as -*ism* and -*tion* as noun forms, -*ed* as a verb form, and -*ly* as an adverb.

Word Form Error in the Written Expression Section

- Remember that suffixes or word forms are the most common type of error tested in the Written Expression section of the TOEFL®.

- In the Written Expression section of the TOEFL®, read the sentence with the four underlined parts A, B, C, and D. Concentrate on the underlined words. Check for errors in word forms.

- The most common type of word form error involves the use of an adjective in place of an adverb or an adverb in place of an adjective.

Note: Adjectives usually answer the question *What kind?* Adjectives modify nouns, noun phrases, and pronouns.

Eleanor Roosevelt was an *influential* first Lady.

- Adverbs usually answer the question *How?* Adverbs modify verbs, adjectives, and participles. Most adverbs are formed by adding *-ly* to the adjective. However, some adjectives also end in *-ly*.

Theodore Roosevelt traveled *extensively*.

- Check for word form errors that include the use of words related to certain fields and the people who work in the field (botany, botanical, a botanist).
- Check for word form errors involving adjectives and nouns (developing/development).
- Check for other word form errors such as a noun in place of a verb (belief/believe).
- If you still cannot find the error, eliminate the options that seem correct. If you have more than one option left, take a guess.

A. Noun Suffixes

These endings will indicate that the words are nouns.

The following suffixes indicate people who do things:

Suffix	*Examples*
–ee	trainee, interviewee
–er	interviewer, employer
–or	translator, demonstrator

The following suffixes describe people:

Suffix	*Examples*
–an, –ian	Mexican, Parisian, historian
–ist	journalist, artist

Other noun suffixes:

Suffix	*Examples*
–age	passage, postage
–al	renewal, arrival
–ance, –ence	acceptance, independence
–dom	freedom, kingdom
–hood	childhood, motherhood
–ion, –sion, –tion	addiction, conclusion, introduction
–ism	materialism, realism
–y, –ity	prosperity, hostility
–ment	entertainment, arrangement
–ness	kindness, greatness
–ship	relationship, courtship
–ure, –sis	failure, diagnosis

EXERCISE 1

Make these verbs into nouns by adding the correct suffix.

1. sign _____
2. close _____
3. insist _____
4. prefer _____
5. exist _____
6. assemble _____
7. deny _____
8. try _____
9. store _____
10. exclude _____
11. persuade _____
12. improve _____
13. acquire _____

14. seize _____
15. obey _____
16. emphasize _____
17. differ _____
18. recover _____
19. prosper _____
20. propose _____
21. shrink _____
22. break _____
23. explode _____
24. encourage _____
25. advertise _____
26. produce _____

B. Adjective Suffixes

The following suffixes indicate adjectives:

Suffix	Examples
–able, –ible	eatable, sensible
–ant, –ent	concordant, prudent
–ary	complimentary
–ic	enigmatic, democratic
–ical	musical, practical
–ish	childish, greenish
–ive	attractive, protective
–like	godlike, childlike
–ly	nightly, scholarly
–ory	sensory, satisfactory
–ous	poisonous, adventurous
–some	handsome, lonesome
–worthy	trustworthy
–y	salty, rainy

The suffixes -*ful* (with) and -*less* (without):

Suffix	Examples
–ful	faithful, dreadful
–less	harmless, careless

Comparative and superlatives:

Suffix	Examples
–er	smaller, longer
–est	smallest, longest

EXERCISE 2

Make the following words into adjectives by adding the correct suffix.

1. week _____
2. humor _____
3. poetry _____
4. grammar _____
5. agree _____
6. talk _____
7. child _____
8. tire _____
9. courage _____
10. hand _____
11. harm _____
12. depend _____
13. inform _____
14. grass _____
15. miracle _____
16. drama _____
17. alphabet _____
18. regret _____
19. create _____
20. boy _____
21. danger _____
22. mouth _____
23. pain _____
24. hesitate _____
25. adjust _____
26. climate _____

C. Adverb Suffixes

The following suffixes indicate adverbs:

Suffix	Examples
–ly	slowly, sharply
–er (comparative)	harder, faster
–est (superlative)	hardest, fastest

D. Verb Suffixes

The following suffixes indicate verbs:

Suffix	*Examples*
–en	strengthen, weaken
–ate	activate, domesticate
–ize	sterilize, tranquilize
–fy, –ify	pacify, purify

 EXERCISE 3

Make the following words into verbs by adding the correct suffix. In some cases you may have to change the spelling of the root word.

1. hospital _____

2. sympathy _____

3. solid _____

4. captive _____

5. fright _____

6. length _____

7. dark _____

8. less _____

9. flat _____

10. bright _____

11. regular _____

12. thick _____

13. false _____

14. identity _____

15. liberty _____

16. sweet _____

17. broad _____

18. immune _____

19. deep _____

 EXERCISE 4

Complete the chart with the appropriate word forms. In some cases there may be more than one answer.

	Verb	Noun	Adjective	Adverb
1.	exclude	exclusion	exclusive	exclusively
2.	_____	repetition	_____	_____
3.	_____	_____	different	_____
4.	_____	_____	_____	electrically
5.	_____	emphasis	_____	_____
6.	_____	_____	economical	_____
7.	decide	_____	_____	_____

Verb	Noun	Adjective	Adverb
8. _____	competition	_____	_____
9. _____	_____	exclusive	_____
10. _____	_____	_____	purely

EXERCISE 5

Complete the chart with the appropriate word forms. In some cases there may be more than one answer.

Verb	Noun	Adjective	Adverb
1. _____	_____	beautiful	_____
2. _____	origin	_____	_____
3. free	_____	_____	_____
4. _____	_____	_____	simply
5. _____	_____	familiar	_____
6. generalize	_____	_____	_____
7. _____	organization	_____	_____
8. _____	_____	_____	originally
9. _____	_____	sanitary	_____
10. succeed	_____	_____	_____

EXERCISE 6

Complete the chart with the appropriate word forms.

Thing/place	Person	Adjective
1. machine	machinist	mechanical
2. art	_____	_____
3. _____	politician	_____
4. _____	_____	musical
5. electricity	_____	_____
6. botany	_____	_____
7. theory	_____	_____
8. _____	poet	_____
9. finance	_____	_____
10. _____	_____	scientific

Test on Suffixes

From the four underlined words or phrases A, B, C, or D, identify the <u>one</u> which is not correct.

EXAMPLE

In recent years, <u>chemical</u> <u>pollutants</u> sucked up by the <u>atmospheric</u> fell back down to earth
               A   B   C

in forms of <u>precipitation</u>.
           D

Choice (C) is the best answer. A noun, <u>atmosphere</u>, should be the object of the verb "sucked up."

1. Some fishes live at such <u>enormous</u> <u>depths</u> that they are almost <u>complete</u> <u>blind</u>.
                          A   B   C   D

2. The <u>reduction</u> of <u>illiteracy</u> is the <u>primary</u> <u>education</u> task in many parts of the world.
      A   B   C   D

3. One of the <u>majority</u> causes of <u>tides</u> is the <u>gravitational</u> <u>attraction</u> of the moon.
           A   B   C   D

4. For the <u>development</u> of a coral reef, <u>warmth</u>, <u>shallow</u>, and <u>clear</u> sea water without any silts or
        A   B   C   D

clays is needed.

5. Many species of lizards change their <u>diets</u> with <u>mature</u> and <u>seasonal</u> changes in the <u>availability</u> of
                                  A   B   C   D

food.

6. James McNeill Whistler, considered as the greatest <u>genius</u> in the history of American art, was a
                                         A

<u>versatility</u> and <u>industrious</u> artist who was <u>proficient</u> in several media.
   B   C   D

7. Animals that live in <u>cold</u> <u>climates</u> often <u>hibernate</u> throughout the winter when food is <u>scarcely</u>.
                 A   B   C   D

8. <u>Severe</u> <u>emotional</u> <u>stress</u> may elicit symptoms of disease that may be <u>latently</u> in the body.
   A   B   C   D

9. Oliver Wendell Holmes, a <u>judge</u> who supported the <u>free</u> of <u>speech</u>, was known for his <u>wit</u>.
                  A   B   C   D

10. Language is an <u>important</u> <u>factor</u> in the <u>accumulate</u> of <u>culture</u>.
            A   B   C   D

11. Frederick Douglass, an <u>escaped</u> slave, became a leading <u>abolition</u> and <u>orator</u>, lecturing for an
                  A   B   C

<u>antislavery</u> society in Massachusetts.
   D

12. Hearing, or <u>audition</u>, is affected by the <u>intensity</u>, <u>frequency</u>, and <u>complex</u> of pressure waves in the
          A   B   C   D

air or other transmitting substances.

13. Dorothea Dix crusaded for the <u>science</u> and <u>humane</u> treatment of the <u>mentally</u> <u>ill</u>.
                        A   B   C   D

14. A mirage is a kind of <u>optical</u> <u>illusion</u> that occurs in <u>heat</u>, <u>still</u> weather.
                   A   B   C D

15. Ralph Waldo Emerson, the <u>writer</u>, stressed the <u>important</u> of <u>individuality</u> and <u>self-reliance</u>.
                 A   B   C   D

CHAPTER 13

Phrasal Verbs

M A K E	U P
T A K E	A F T E R
K E E P	U P W I T H

Some verbs are *made up* of more than one word. We call these two-word, or three-word verbs, or phrasal verbs. The combination of words that *make up* phrasal verbs have a very different meaning from the meanings of the words taken separately. MAKE has a meaning and UP has a meaning, but when we use these words together the combination has a completely different meaning. In this case MAKE UP means to compose.

Phrasal verbs are very common in English, especially in the spoken language. In the TOEFL® they appear not only in the Listening Comprehension section, but in the other sections as well. This chapter will help you recognize and learn a number of phrasal verbs and their meanings.

Reading Practice

Read the following passage.

Charles Richter and his family left their Ohio farm in 1908 and headed for Los Angeles. In less than a year they felt their first earthquake, which so impressed nine-year-old Richter that he ended up dedicating his life to earthquake research.

After completing his education in Los Angeles area schools, Richter signed up at the University of Southern California, and a year later moved to northern California and attended Stanford University. He graduated from Stanford in 1920, then earned a Ph.D. in Physics from Caltech in Pasadena in 1928. While Richter was at Caltech he was offered a job in the school's seismology lab where he and the lab's director, Dr. Beno Gutenberg, soon got busy on a new project that would keep track of southern California earthquakes. They divided the quakes into categories to which they gave numerical values called magnitudes. Using instruments known as seismographs, Gutenberg and Richter in 1935 worked out a scale for measuring earthquakes. Today it is well known as the Richter scale.

 EXERCISE 1

Work with a partner, with a group, or alone to answer the following questions.

1. What did Charles Richter and his family do in 1908?

Task

Discuss the difference in meaning of the following phrasal verbs:

head for   head on   head out

Use a dictionary to check your answers.

2. Does "ended up" in sentence 2 mean Richter stopped his earthquake research?

Task

Find three different possibilities for the following person's future.

John is a high school student who excels in math and English. He is also a star football player. What may John end up doing?

3. In order to study at the University of Southern California, what did Richter have to do?

Task

Name one thing that you can

sign on _____   **sign up** _____   **sign out** _____

4. What did Dr. Gutenberg and Charles Richter do in 1935?

Task

Write three phrasal verbs using the main verb above. How are their meanings different?

 ## EXERCISE 2

Work with a partner, with a group, or alone. Read the following conversation. Then complete the conversation using phrasal verbs from the list below. Use each word only one time. The first one has been done for you.

sit down	stop by	set up	pack up
pick up	look after	take off	

Bob: Is everything <u>set up</u> for our picnic?

Tina: We're ready but Brenda called a few minutes ago and said she and Carlos still have a few

        things to _____ at the store.

Bob: Did she tell you when they would be here?

Tina: Yes, they'll be coming by in about an hour.

Bob: What do you want to do while we wait?

Tina: I'd like to _____ and rest for a while.

Bob: How could you be tired? It's not noon yet!

Tina: Well I had to _____ all these picnic items and _____ my little

        brother too.

Bob: Of course. I'm sorry I didn't _____ earlier to help you, but I've been busy all

        morning.

Tina: That's all right. I'll relax at the lake this afternoon.

Bob: Well, we'd better get busy and put these things in the car. Brenda and Carlos will be here soon

        and we want to be able to _____ right away.

STRATEGIES

- Since the meaning of some phrasal verbs are not clear from the individual words that make them up, it is important to recognize and learn as many as you can.
- If you do not know a phrasal verb that is used idiomatically, you can work out its meaning from the context.

---

sign up

He *signed up* for the new computer course at the college.

From the context of "the college" and "the computer course," we can work out that "signed up" means enrolled.

- *The Grammar of Phrasal Verbs:* Some phrasal verbs can be separated, other phrasal verbs cannot be separated. Phrasal verbs consist of a verb and a preposition or a verb and an adverb.

Some phrasal verbs have no object.   Other phrasal verbs have objects.

EXAMPLE   EXAMPLE

The lights went out suddenly.   He turned on the light.*

Look out!   I looked for my keys.*

* With these phrasal verbs you must be careful where you put the object. The object of most separable phrasal verbs can be put either after the verb or after the preposition/adverb.

EXAMPLE

He turned on <u>the light</u>.   or   He turned <u>the light</u> on.
        object   object

The object of an inseparable phrasal verb can only be put in one place—after the preposition/adverb.

EXAMPLE

I looked for <u>my keys</u>.   (Not: I looked my keys for)
        object

A good dictionary will tell you the meaning of a phrasal verb and where to put the object.

A verb combined with one or two prepositions or adverbs can have a variety of meanings. Look at the verb COME and its many meanings below.

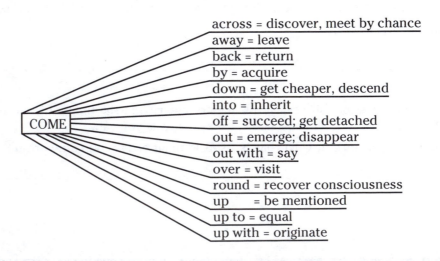

COME	across = discover, meet by chance
	away = leave
	back = return
	by = acquire
	down = get cheaper, descend
	into = inherit
	off = succeed; get detached
	out = emerge; disappear
	out with = say
	over = visit
	round = recover consciousness
	up = be mentioned
	up to = equal
	up with = originate

EXERCISE 3

Complete the meanings of the phrasal verbs in the diagram below. Use a dictionary to check your answers.

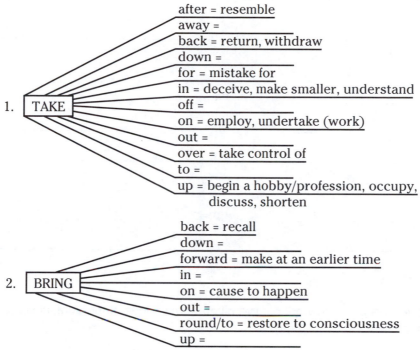

1. **TAKE**
   - after = resemble
   - away = _____
   - back = return, withdraw
   - down = _____
   - for = mistake for
   - in = deceive, make smaller, understand
   - off = _____
   - on = employ, undertake (work)
   - out = _____
   - over = take control of
   - to = _____
   - up = begin a hobby/profession, occupy, discuss, shorten

2. **BRING**
   - back = recall
   - down = _____
   - forward = make at an earlier time
   - in = _____
   - on = cause to happen
   - out = _____
   - round/to = restore to consciousness
   - up = _____

 EXERCISE 4

Work with a partner or a group to work out the different meanings of the phrasal verbs below. Then check in your dictionary to see if you were correct.

Meaning

BE

about to = _____   over = _____

after = _____   up = _____

behind = _____   up against = _____

off = _____   up and about = _____

on to = _____   up to = _____

out for = _____

out of = _____

EXERCISE 5

Work with a partner or a group to work out the different meanings of the phrasal verbs below. Then check in a dictionary to see if you were correct.

Meaning

TURN

away = _____	off = _____
back = _____	on = _____
down = _____	out = _____
in = _____	over = _____
into = _____	up = _____

EXERCISE 6

Work with a partner or a group to work out five different meanings of the phrasal verbs with MAKE and GET. Check your answers in a dictionary.

MAKE

1. _____
2. _____
3. _____
4. _____
5. _____

GET

1. _____
2. _____
3. _____
4. _____
5. _____

Phrasal Verb Practice

The following section will not only help you with the Reading and Vocabulary Section of the TOEFL® test, but will also help to increase your vocabulary in general. Use a dictionary to look up words you do not know in the multiple choice items.

EXERCISE **1**

Choose the one answer that could best replace the underlined phrasal verb without changing the meaning of the sentence.

EXAMPLE

In the game of soccer, the rule <u>setting down</u> 11 members to a side went into effect in 1870.

    (A) depositing
    (B) directing
    (C) stipulating
    (D) installing

The best answer is (C) because "In the game of soccer, the rule stipulating 11 members to a side went into effect in 1870" is closest in meaning to the original sentence.

1. Ultrasonic sound waves can <u>pick out</u> cracks in metal that the human eye cannot see.
    (A) choose
    (B) dissect
    (C) detect
    (D) restore

2. The porcupine fish <u>blows up</u> its body with water when it is alarmed.
    (A) bursts
    (B) exaggerates
    (C) magnifies
    (D) inflates

3. During World War I in the United States, posters were used to ask young men to <u>sign up</u> in a serious campaign to fight the enemy.
    (A) enlist
    (B) fire
    (C) testify
    (D) write

4. The unmanned U.S. space probe Mariner 9 <u>sent back</u> over 7,000 photos of Mars.
    (A) circulated
    (B) transmitted
    (C) conferred
    (D) submitted

5. A government's economic resources must not be <u>used up</u>.
    (A) deposited
    (B) conditioned
    (C) depleted
    (D) devoured

6. In 1955, the Rosa Parks incident in Alabama <u>set off</u> a year-long bus boycott by African-Americans.
    (A) sparked
    (B) forced
    (C) detonated
    (D) isolated

7. In the 1980s TV viewers began to <u>hook up</u> videocassette players to their TVs.
    (A) combine
    (B) connect
    (C) fasten
    (D) blend

8. For centuries people <u>made up</u> stories about dragons.
    (A) constructed
    (B) beautified
    (C) created
    (D) prepared

9. The work was <u>singled out</u> to receive an award at the exhibition.
    (A) impressed
    (B) subscribed
    (C) cautioned
    (D) marked

10. The rate of inflation in the United States has not <u>gone up and down</u> more than 10 percent in the 1980s.
    (A) fluctuated
    (B) hesitated
    (C) alternated
    (D) lingered

Phrasal Verb Practice

Phrasal verbs are often tested in the Structure and Written Expression section of the TOEFL® test.

EXAMPLE

Of the four underlined parts of the sentences marked (A), (B), (C), and (D), choose the one word or phrase that must be changed for the sentence to be correct.

Sir George Everest, the surveyor general of India, was <u>the first</u> to <u>take in</u> the
                                                          A   B

detailed <u>mapping of</u> India, including <u>the Himalayas</u>.
         D   E

The sentence should read "Sir George Everest, the surveyor general of India, was the first to take on the detailed mapping of India, including the Himalayas." Therefore, you should choose (B) as the incorrect answer.

The following exercises will help you to practice for this section of the test.

EXERCISE 2

In the following sentences the underlined phrasal verbs may or may not be correct. Write C if they are correct, or write the correct form if they are not correct.

_____ 1. When the American War of Independence <u>broke up</u>, George Washington was appointed commander in chief of the American forces.

_____ 2. Christopher Columbus discovered Cuba and the island of Hispaniola where he <u>set up</u> a colony.

_____ 3. Clothing factories <u>sprang off</u> during the Industrial Revolution around the latter part of the 18th century.

_____ 4. Jane Addams was a social worker who <u>stood out for</u> women's rights and social reforms for the poor.

_____ 5. After the British captured New Amsterdam, they changed its name to New York and <u>took out</u> the wall around it.

_____ 6. To forecast possible tsunamis, warning stations with seismographic equipment to <u>follow up</u> and record earthquakes have been <u>set out</u>.

_____ 7. Flying fish <u>work out</u> speed with their tails just below the surface, and leap clear of the water to avoid their enemies.

_____ 8. Red corpuscles which carry oxygen through the blood <u>wear out</u> within a few weeks and are remade in the bone marrow.

_____ 9. The possum will roll over on its side and play dead to <u>put on</u> the attacker.

_____ 10. In 1972 five men <u>broke into</u> the Watergate building and <u>put in</u> listening devices.

More Phrasal Verb Practice

Phrasal verbs appear in the reading passages of the TOEFL® test. Knowing their meaning will help you understand the passage and answer the vocabulary questions.

EXERCISE 1

Underline the phrasal verbs in the following reading passage:

In the spring of 1856 a herd of camels was brought to Texas, as a result of encouragement by Jefferson Davis, Secretary of War. It was hoped that the camels might clear up some of the transportation problems, especially across the desert areas where water was scarce, and where horses and mules suffered severely. Experimentation under the command of Lieutenant Beale showed that the camels would carry heavy loads long distances without water and reach their destination in good condition. Beale took a camel brigade across the southern trails to California and showed his animals off in Los Angeles in January, 1858. Various factors, however, prevented the experiment from going on further. Horse and mule teams were badly frightened by the camels and the outbreak of the Civil War put off interest.

Year by year the number of camels in the Texas herd decreased; many of the animals wandered away; and later, in one manner or another the herds were dispersed.

EXERCISE 2

Fill in the blanks with one of the following words. You may use some words more than once.

up	out	part	on

The Iroquois tribe of American Indians in pre-colonial times took _____ in a very special form of government. The League Council headed the social structure, being made _____ of a set number of members from each of the tribes. The council members were called "sachems." A sachem would take _____ this position through the family. The head mother, together with other women in her family would pick _____ the sachem. The women also had the power to dismiss the sachem from the council if they thought he was not carrying _____ his duties properly.

EXERCISE 3

Fill in the blanks with the words in the boxes below. You may use some words more than once.

spread	up	were	with	from
throught	out	of		

A. In November 1988, a computer "virus" _____ through business, military, and university computers. A set of instructions was _____ up that would duplicate itself and go _____ computer to computer through networks of discs that were shared. The virus filled _____ the memory capacity of 60,000 computers that were hooked _____ _____ the Internet network. The computers ran _____ _____ memory and soon _____ _____ _____ operation.

up	placed	passed	out	through
turned	pulled	found		

B. In July 1976, 29 American Legion conventioneers died of a mysterious disease in Philadelphia. Another 50 conventioneers became ill but _____ _____. In 1977, the disease which became known as "Legionnaires' disease" _____ _____ to be caused by a bacteria; however, no one has ever _____ _____ how the Legionnaires got infected. There was speculation that the bacteria could have been _____ on through the air vents of the hotel where the convention took _____. Since 1976 other cases of the disease have _____ _____.

set	with	stand	up
out	about	brought	

C. William Randolph Hearst was a journalist and publisher who _____ up a huge publishing empire that included 18 newspapers and nine magazines. Hearst was the first journalist who started "sensational" newspaper reporting. Reporters for his newspapers would make an event much more dramatic than it really was so that people would buy Hearst's newspapers. The articles were also backed _____ _____ photos that made the drama _____ _____ even more. Articles in Hearst's newspapers about the alleged mistreatment of Cuban citizens by Spanish soldiers began to stir _____ public hatred against the Spanish. This then _____ _____ the U.S. military involvement in the Spanish-American War.

Test 1: Phrasal Verbs

Read the following passage and answer the questions on phrasal verbs.

A shoal of piranhas can <u>tear up</u> the carcass of a dead cow to its bones in just a few minutes. But it is surprising to <u>find out</u> that these fish also eat fruit and nuts. Sometimes a shoal of piranhas waits under the branches of a rubber tree for the seeds to <u>pop out</u> of the pods. The seeds are then <u>gobbled up</u> even before they reach the ground. Many other species of fish have <u>caught on</u> to fruit and nut eating like the piranhas. By following the flood waters of the Amazon each rainy season the fish live in the forest in shallow water and even <u>put on</u> fat to <u>live through</u> the period when the water <u>moves away</u>. Researchers at the *Instituto de Pesquisas da Amazonia* have found that several species of piranhas have <u>given up</u> meat eating and turned into vegetarians.

Choose the answer that could best replace the underlined phrasal verbs without changing the meaning of the sentence.

1. tear up
   - (A) slice
   - (B) amputate
   - (C) shred
   - (D) carve

2. find out
   - (A) discover
   - (B) distinguish
   - (C) discern
   - (D) explore

3. pop out of
   - (A) protrude from
   - (B) burst from
   - (C) hop from
   - (D) plunge from

4. gobbled up
   - (A) stuffed
   - (B) digested
   - (C) eaten
   - (D) liquified

5. caught on
   - (A) reversed
   - (B) transformed
   - (C) adapted
   - (D) exchanged

6. put on
   - (A) worn
   - (B) extended
   - (C) attached
   - (D) added

7. live through
   - (A) dwell
   - (B) survive
   - (C) experience
   - (D) suffer

8. moves away
   - (A) subsides
   - (B) shrinks
   - (C) recedes
   - (D) abandons

9. given up
   - (A) ceded
   - (B) yielded
   - (C) concluded
   - (D) ceased

Test 2: Phrasal Verbs

From the four choices below each sentence, select the word or phrase that could best replace the underlined phrasal verb without changing the meaning of the sentence.

1. Different kinds of beads are used to ward off evil.
   - (A) avert
   - (B) conduce
   - (C) anticipate
   - (D) restrain

2. A nerve is made up of a bundle of nerve fibers.
   - (A) conceived
   - (B) produced
   - (C) consumed
   - (D) composed

3. After the Ice Age many species of animals <u>died out</u>.
   (A) froze
   (B) receded
   (C) became extinct
   (D) became extinguished

4. With present day technology it has been possible to locate the exact spot where the famous ship, the *Titanic,* <u>went down</u>.
   (A) faded
   (B) sank
   (C) slumped
   (D) diminished

5. There are about 200 grizzly bears in Yellowstone Park and the population is <u>going down</u> by an estimated four percent each year.
   (A) declining
   (B) decaying
   (C) succumbing
   (D) submerging

6. A brief outline of the course and bibliography were <u>handed out</u> to the students at the first meeting.
   (A) dispensed
   (B) dispersed
   (C) distributed
   (D) contributed

7. The brain <u>uses up</u> 25 percent of the oxygen you breathe in.
   (A) handles
   (B) consumes
   (C) adopts
   (D) exhausts

8. Certain wild animals are weighed and studied before the effect of the tranquilizer <u>wears off</u>.
   (A) decays
   (B) removes
   (C) leaves
   (D) shrinks

9. It is uncertain that salaries can <u>keep up</u> with the rate of inflation.
   (A) restore
   (B) reduce
   (C) encounter
   (D) maintain

10. Talks over the persisting war <u>broke down</u> as they could not reach an agreement.
    (A) cracked
    (B) failed
    (C) smashed
    (D) were interrupted

11. In the 17th century the idea of drinking chocolate <u>caught on</u> in Europe.
    (A) became disliked
    (B) became dangerous
    (C) became popular
    (D) became questionable

12. The popular story that George Washington admitted to his father that he had <u>cut down</u> a cherry tree is probably an invention.
    (A) severed
    (B) damaged
    (C) mowed
    (D) felled

13. In 1874 Remington <u>came out with</u> the first pratical commercial typewriter.
    (A) considered
    (B) produced
    (C) weighed
    (D) examined

14. The United States <u>turns out</u> 16.5 billion hot dogs each year.
    (A) produces
    (B) controls
    (C) returns
    (D) delivers

15. The Food and Agricultural Organization has <u>worked out</u> how the calorie intake of people compares with what they need for good health.
    (A) calculated
    (B) attacked
    (C) divided
    (D) checked

Answer Key

Chapter 1: Words in Context

Biology Reading

Exercise 1
1. a
2. a
3. b
4. a
5. b
6. b
7. b
8. a
9. b
10. b

Exercise 2
A.
1. den
2. burrow
3. hive
4. den
5. web
6. sty
7. stable
8. nest

B. Answers will vary.

Exercise 3
1. b
2. e
3. g
4. c
5. a
6. d
7. b
8. f

Science Reading

Exercise 1
1. a
2. a
3. b
4. a
5. b
6. a
7. a
8. b

Exercise 2
1. grain
2. comet
3. sky
4. land

Exercise 3
1. grain
2. blade
3. speck
4. breath
5. flake
6. item
7. fragment
8. trace

Exercise 4
1. meteor
2. earth
3. star
4. solar system
5. galaxy
6. universe

Reading about People

Exercise 1
1. a
2. b
3. a
4. a
5. a
6. b
7. b
8. a

Exercise 2
A.
1. b
2. a
3. c
4. b
5. c
6. b
7. a
8. b
9. c

B. Answers will vary.

Exercise 3
1. start
2. improve
3. teach

Reading on Social Science

Exercise 1
1. a
2. b
3. b
4. a
5. a
6. b
7. a
8. b

Exercise 2
A.

Dry	Not Dry
arid	damp
dessicated	humid
baked	saturated
parched	immersed
	soaked
	moist

B. Answers will vary.

Exercise 3

Synonyms	Antonyms
1. plentiful	scarce
2. abundant	meager
3. overflowing	skimpy
4. profuse	scant
5. bountiful	limited

Exercise 4
1. reservation
2. neighbors
3. hunting
4. tribe

History Reading

Exercise 1
1. a
2. b
3. a
4. b
5. b

Exercise 2
1. dwarf
2. infinitesimal
3. minute
4. memorial

Exercise 3
A.

Newspaper	Book
column	bibliography
article	appendix
editorial	index
headline	biography
	glossary

B. Answers will vary.

Exercise 4

1. comprise   3. erect   5. bind
2. establish   4. occur   6. lift

Reading on Earthquakes

Exercise 1

1. a   3. b   5. a
2. a   4. a   6. b

Exercise 2

A.

Feelings	Your Leg	Your Reputation
hurt	injure	hurt
	hurt	harm
		damage
		destroy

A Painting	The Environment	Your Health
mar	damage	impair
damage	harm	harm
destroy	spoil	destroy
spoil	destroy	

B. Answers will vary.

Exercise 3

A.

Continuous Sound	Single Sound
roar	crack
rumble	squeak
rattle	bang
hum	slam
rustle	
murmur	

B. Answers will vary.

Exercise 4

1. b   3. a   5. b
2. b   4. b   6. a

Exercise 5

1. a   3. a   5. b
2. b   4. b

Exercise 6

A.

1. b   3. a   5. f
2. d   4. c   6. e

B. Answers will vary.

Science Reading

Exercise 1

1. b   3. a   5. b
2. a   4. b   6. a

Exercise 2

A.

False	Fake	Counterfeit
teeth	flowers	money
impression	smile	letters
alarm	diamonds	
statement	painting	
address		

Phoney	Artificial
address	flowers
smile	sweetener
	smile

B. Answers will vary.

Exercise 3

1. secretion = release of a material formed by an animal or plant
2. resin = a natural organic substance used chiefly in varnishes, printing inks, plastics, and medicines
3. extract = a product prepared by something withdrawn (such as a juice) by a physical or chemical process
4. fluid = a substance that flows or conforms to the outline of its container

Exercise 4

1. copy   3. a product
2. compound

Science Reading

Exercise 1

1. b   3. a   5. b
2. b   4. b   6. a

Exercise 2

1. hit   3. television
2. space   4. orbit

Exercise 3

1. trail   3. course
2. orbit   4. circuit

Exercise 4

Synonyms	Antonyms
1. transmit	pick up
2. send out	obtain
3. relay	record
4. give	accept
5. convey	acquire
6. dispatch	receive

Reading on Literature

Exercise 1

1. b   4. b   7. a
2. b   5. b
3. a   6. a

Exercise 2

1. an epic   6. prose
2. a poet   7. a rhyme
3. a chronicle   8. a nursery rhyme
4. a lyric   9. a monologue
5. verse   10. dialogue

Exercise 3

1. abridgement   3. accompaniment
2. accomplished   4. history

Archeology Reading

Exercise 1

1. a   5. a
2. b   6. b
3. a   7. a
4. b   8. a

Exercise 2

1. c   3. a   5. e, f
2. e   4. b   6. g

Exercise 3

Synonyms	Antonyms
1. accurate	incorrect
2. exact	mistaken
3. perfect	flawed

4. precise   faulty
5. definite   mistaken

Exercise 4
1. country
2. building
3. city
4. botanist

Exercise 5

Decay	Rot
buildings	apples
teeth	flesh
a statue	trees
society	tomatoes
standards	wood

Exercise 6
1. To dehydrate—to remove water from
2. To pickle—to put in vinegar and salt water
3. To preserve—to add sugar and put in a jar
4. To can—to seal in an airtight container
5. To smoke—to cook in the smoke of burning hardwood

Sample TOEFL® Test 1

Exercise 1
1. B   3. C   5. B
2. A   4. D   6. A

Exercise 2
A.
1. tricolor
2. quintuplets
3. unicycle
4. century
5. pentagon
6. sexagenarian
7. decathlon
8. monotone
9. bimonthly
10. quadruple

B. Answers will vary.

Sample TOEFL® Test 2

Exercise 1
1. B   3. A   5. B
2. C   4. C   6. D

Exercise 2

Rock	Tree
molten rock	genealogical tree
rock oil	tree house
rock fall	tree line
rock-bound	tree frog
rock salt	tree farm
rock candy	banana tree
rock crystal	vascular tree
rockweed	
rockrose	
pervious rock	

Sample TOEFL® Test 3

Exercise 1
1. C   3. A   5. A
2. D   4. B   6. D

Exercise 2
A.
2. Silurian
4. Carboniferous
6. Cretaceous
8. Triassic

B. Rocks

Exercise 3
1. drained
2. rough
3. ancient
4. superficially
5. to receive

Chapter 2: Theme Grouping: Living Things

Exercise 1
1. The settlers
2. wild and seedling trees
3. an outer leathery husk
4. an inner shell

Exercise 2
1. No, Sonja is an immigrant.
2. Betty and Tom are colleagues; that is, they work together.
3. Sonja is enjoying southern California. As a matter of fact, she feels like a native.
4. You can't eat the rind of a pomegranate, just the flesh around the seeds.
5. Betty will bring Sonja some blossoms from her rose garden.

A. Types of Inhabitants

Exercise 1
1. F   5. F
2. F   6. F
3. T   7. T
4. F   8. T

Exercise 2
1. a   5. b
2. b   6. c
3. a   7. b
4. c   8. c

B. The Life of Plants

Exercise 1
1. seedling   4. bloom   7. wither
2. shoot   5. wilt
3. bud   6. droop

Exercise 2
1. b   4. b   7. b
2. c   5. c   8. b
3. a   6. a   9. b

C. Parts of a Fruit or Nut

Exercise 1
1. F   5. T
2. F   6. T
3. T   7. T
4. T   8. F

Exercise 2
1. c   4. c   7. c
2. c   5. b   8. a
3. a   6. a   9. c

Test on Living Things
1. B   5. C   9. C
2. A   6. C   10. C
3. C   7. A   11. D
4. B   8. B   12. A

Chapter 3: Theme Grouping: Time and Space

Exercise 1
1. The Great Plains region has frequently been subject to periodic drought.
2. The grassland and crops were scorched.

3. The topsoil was parched and blown away by the wind.
4. The soil was rich and fertile before it dried up and was blown away.
5. The area was named the "Dust Bowl."

Exercise 2
1. Julie travels to Africa frequently.
2. Julie prepares for her trips prior to departure.
3. Her final destination is Mount Kilimanjaro.
4. The weather will be balmy for the most part.
5. The savannas will be arid.
6. The heat will be scorching.
7. It will be quite chilly on Kilimanjaro.
8. Malindi will be sultry and humid.
9. In the Rift Valley the grass is parched.

A. Adverbs of Time
Exercise 1
1. T	5. F
2. F	6. T
3. T	7. T
4. T	8. F

Exercise 2
1. b	6. b
2. b	7. b
3. a	8. c
4. a	9. c
5. c	10. b

B. Dry and Not Dry
Exercise 1
1. T	5. T
2. T	6. F
3. F	7. T
4. T	8. F

Exercise 2
1. b	6. a
2. a	7. c
3. a	8. b
4. c	9. b
5. b	10. b

C. Hot and Not Hot
Exercise 1
1. F	5. T
2. F	6. F
3. T	7. T
4. T	8. T

Exercise 2
1. b	6. b
2. a	7. c
3. a	8. b
4. a	9. a
5. c	10. b

Test on Time and Space
1. C	5. C	9. B
2. B	6. A	10. C
3. C	7. A	11. C
4. A	8. C	

Chapter 4: Everyday and Specific Vocabulary
Exercise 1
1. The conversation is taking place at the library.

2. Carol is doing research for her term paper.
3. Lisa attended one of Dr. Kent's seminars.
4. The seminar was held in the auditorium on campus.
5. Lisa has registered for one of Dr. Kent's classes.
6. Carol thinks Dr. Kent is a good instructor.
7. Carol has two more resources to find before the library closes.
8. Lisa has to study for her history final.
9. They will see each other during semester break.

Exercise 2
1. The health care program provides complete medical care.
2. The hospital coverage includes nursing and physician's care, surgery, therapy, laboratory tests, and medicines.
3. Benefits include regular checkups, and vision and hearing examinations.
4. More than 90 medical offices provide routine care, as well as lab, pharmacy, and X-ray services.
5. The well-trained medical staff and specialists will give the best treatment available.

Identifying Locations
Exercise 1
A. Bank
1. withdrawal
2. deposit slip
3. balance

B. Restaurant
1. dressing
2. house special
3. tip

C. Garage
1. tune-up
2. brake fluid
3. radiator

D. School
1. tuition
2. registration
3. schedule of classes

E. Supermarket
1. aisle
2. deli
3. produce

F. Clothing Store
1. sales attendant
2. charge account
3. exchange

G. Theater
1. box office
2. row
3. usher

H. Post Office
1. special delivery
2. registered
3. money order

I. Courtroom
1. jury
2. case
3. prosecutor

J. Library
1. reference
2. periodicals
3. nonfiction

K. On a Bus
1. schedule
2. fare
3. transfer

L. Zoo
1. feeding time
2. cages
3. aviary

Exercise 2
A. gas station attendant	B. dentist
C. plumber	D. apartment manager
E. police officer	F. nurse
G. car salesperson	H. travel agent
I. college student	J. electrician

Test on Everyday and Specific Vocabulary
1. C	6. A	11. B
2. B	7. A	12. B
3. C	8. D	13. D
4. D	9. C	14. A
5. B	10. C	15. D

Chapter 5: Roots

Exercise 1
1. Some theories of laughter emphasize its ability to reduce tension and emotion.
2. Laughter produces a beneficial biological response.
3. When you laugh at a problem, you are putting it in a new perspective.

Exercise 2
1. ab<u>dic</u>ate
2. pro<u>spect</u>
3. <u>creed</u>
4. e<u>vid</u>ent

A. Root: *Cred*

Exercise 1
1. b
2. a
3. b
4. a
5. b
6. a
7. b

Exercise 2
1. accredited
2. incredulity
3. discreditable
4. credit
5. incredulous
6. creed
7. credence
8. credible

B. Roots: *Spect, Spec*

Exercise 1
1. spectators
2. aspect
3. perspective
4. retrospect
5. a respected
6. specimen
7. spectrum
8. spectacle

Exercise 2
1. spectacle
2. retrospect
3. spectrum
4. perspective
5. aspect
6. spectator
7. respected person
8. specimen

C. Roots: *Duc, Duct*

Exercise 1
1. f
2. g
3. h
4. a
5. c
6. d
7. b
8. e

Exercise 2
1. b
2. a
3. b
4. b
5. b
6. a
7. b
8. a

D. Roots: *Ced, Cess*

Exercise 1
1. antecedent
2. precedent
3. recede
4. successive
5. concede
6. process
7. procedure
8. secede

Exercise 2
1. b
2. b
3. a
4. b
5. a
6. b

Exercise 3
Answers will vary.

Exercise 4
1. mostly, chiefly
2. capitivate, appeal to, draw attention from
3. to make sounds
4. birds

Exercise 5
1. the study of humans in relation to culture and environment
2. graphologist
3. astronomer
4. reasoning from a part to a whole, from particulars to generals
5. chronological

Test on Roots
1. C
2. D
3. B
4. D
5. B
6. A
7. D
8. A
9. B
10. C
11. D
12. A

Chapter 6: Theme Grouping: Thought and Communication

Exercise 1
1. The coyote is widespread and can be found from Alaska to New York.
2. Several groups of coyotes singing have a haunting effect.
3. The haunting effect of the songs of several groups over the countryside is unique.

Exercise 2
1. Regina is reflecting on life.
2. Thinking about the future is familiar to Scott.
3. Regina will have to make some crucial decisions.
4. Regina would like to do something unique.
5. "Odd" means unusual.

A. Thinking and Remembering

Exercise 1
1. T
2. T
3. T
4. F
5. T
6. F
7. T
8. F

Exercise 2
1. c
2. c
3. a
4. a
5. b
6. c
7. a
8. b
9. a
10. c

B. Important and Not Important

Exercise 1
1. T
2. T
3. F
4. T
5. F
6. T
7. F
8. F
9. T
10. T

Exercise 2
1. a
2. c
3. a
4. b
5. c
6. c
7. a
8. c
9. b
10. a

C. Usual and Unusual

Exercise 1
1. T
2. F
3. T
4. F
5. T
6. F
7. T
8. T

Exercise 2

1. c	6. c
2. a	7. b
3. a	8. a
4. c	9. b
5. a	10. b

Test on Thought and Communication

1. C	6. B
2. B	7. C
3. D	8. B
4. B	9. A
5. C	10. D

Chapter 7: Theme Grouping: Feelings and Sensations

Exercise 1

1. Americans are not the least bit daring.
2. Seaweed is used in hundreds of prepared foods, from ice cream to salad dressing.
3. No, because cutting the kelp actually helps it grow.

Exercise 2

1. John thought Roberta was looking a little apprehensive.
2. Roberta thinks John is very considerate.
3. Roberta is not as bold as she thought she would be.
4. The lemonade is sour but cold.
5. Roberta thinks John is very generous.

A. Kindness and Unkindness

Exercise 1

1. T	5. F
2. T	6. F
3. T	7. T
4. F	8. F

Exercise 2

1. c	6. c
2. c	7. b
3. a	8. c
4. c	9. a
5. a	10. b

B. Fear and Courage

Exercise 1

1. F	6. F
2. T	7. T
3. F	8. T
4. T	9. T
5. T	10. F

Exercise 2

1. c	6. a
2. a	7. b
3. b	8. c
4. b	9. a
5. c	10. c

C. Types of Taste

Exercise 1

1. F	5. F
2. F	6. T
3. T	7. T
4. T	8. T

Exercise 2

1. c	4. c	7. c
2. a	5. b	8. a
3. a	6. a	9. b

Test on Feelings and Sensations

1. A	5. C	9. D
2. A	6. D	10. B
3. B	7. A	11. A
4. B	8. A	12. D

Chapter 8: Idioms and Confusing Words

Exercise 1

1. No, Mark will not go to the movies because he has to finish his term paper.
2. "Out of the question" means it will not even be considered.

Exercise 2

1. It is not likely they will see whooping cranes.
2. "Few and far between" means not occurring very often.

Exercise 3

1. Yes, since Tom studied hard, it is likely he did well on his exam.
2. "Have a hunch" means to have an idea or feeling about something.

Exercise 4

1. No, Joan met Paul unexpectedly.
2. Paul's plans to go skiing "fell through"; that is, they did not come to pass.
3. Paul will feel "like a fish out of water" because he will be the only male among four females.
4. Joan thinks it is time for Paul to make some new friends.
5. Paul can help them with their homework.
6. Paul had an idea there might be another reason why his cousin asked him to dinner.

A. Idioms

Exercise 1

1. about to	5. out of
2. be on the safe side	6. on my own
3. old hand	7. As a rule
4. above all	8. tired of

Exercise 2

1. c	5. a
2. a	6. a
3. b	7. c
4. c	8. a

Exercise 3

1. C	5. C
2. C	6. I
3. I	7. I
4. C	8. I

Exercise 4

1. feel up to	5. fall behind
2. every other	6. figure out
3. for good	7. fell through
4. a fish out of water	8. feel like

Exercise 5

1. a	5. c
2. c	6. a
3. b	7. b
4. b	8. a

Exercise 6
1. I
2. C
3. I
4. I
5. I
6. C
7. C
8. I

Exercise 7
1. a
2. a
3. b
4. c
5. a
6. c
7. c
8. b

Exercise 8
1. once in a blue moon
2. on the blink
3. on the tip of my tongue
4. pick up the tab
5. piece of cake
6. play it by ear
7. on the right track
8. pull it off

Exercise 9
1. I
2. C
3. I
4. C
5. I
6. I
7. C
8. C

Exercise 10
1. under the weather
2. without a hitch
3. throw cold water on
4. with flying colors
5. take a break
6. straightened up
7. well worth the trouble
8. think nothing of it

Test for Idioms
1. c
2. c
3. b
4. a
5. d
6. a
7. b
8. d
9. b
10. a
11. c
12. d
13. b
14. c
15. a

B.   Confusing Words
Exercise 1
A.
1. b
2. a
3. a
4. b
5. c
6. a
7. b
8. b
9. b
10. b
11. b
12. c
13. b
14. a
15. b
16. b
17. b
18. c
19. b
20. a

B.   Answers will vary.

Exercise 2

She Made	She Did
a confession	her best
a prediction	her duty
a difference	research
a distinction	a report
a contribution	a job
amends	without
way	
an escape	
plans	
progress	
room	
a conclusion	
improvement	
an examination	

Exercise 3
1. made
2. makes
3. Making
4. made
5. made
6. did
7. made
8. made
9. made

Exercise 4
1. Like
2. Like
3. Unlike
4. Like
5. like
6. alike
7. Like
8. Unlike
9. unlike

Test on Confusing Words
1. I
2. C
3. I
4. I
5. I
6. I
7. I
8. I
9. C
10. I
11. I
12. C
13. I
14. C
15. I

Chapter 9:   Prefixes
Exercise 1
1. A tepee could be put up or disassembled in minutes.
2. "Multipurpose" means many purposes.
3. The word "external" tells that the poles were on the outside.
4. The sides could be reattached at the bottom in winter.
5. "Circumference of the tepee" means all the way around the outside.
6. A tribe relocated when resources were depleted.
7. A drag, or *travois,* was a carrier made from tepee poles and a tepee cover rolled up and placed over the poles.
8. Hundreds of people could proceed quickly across the roughest kind of country.

Exercise 2
1. expedition, return
2. renowned
3. circumnavigated
4. detached, regenerate
5. detect
6. transportation
7. produce
8. multicolored

A.   Words Beginning with *De-*
Exercise 1
1. F
2. T
3. T
4. F
5. T
6. T
7. F
8. T

Exercise 2
1. depleted
2. detected
3. decomposes
4. degenerate
5. deviate
6. deflated
7. dehydrate
8. depreciates

B.   Words Beginning with *Inter-*
Exercise 1
1. T
2. T
3. T
4. F
5. F
6. F
7. F
8. F

Exercise 2
1. intermittent
2. intermediate
3. intervened
4. intercepted
5. interact
6. interrelated
7. interspersed
8. intermingled

C.   Words Beginning with *Pro-*
Exercise 1
1. profound
2. proliferate
3. prominent
4. promote
5. protrude
6. prospective
7. proficient
8. proclaim
9. profuse

Exercise 2

1. profuse
2. promote
3. profound
4. prominent
5. prospective
6. proliferate
7. proclaimed
8. protruding
9. proficient

D. Words Beginning with *Dis-*
Exercise 1
1. T
2. F
3. T
4. T
5. T
6. F
7. T
8. T

Exercise 2
1. disparity
2. disinterested
3. dissuade
4. disorient
5. disprove
6. disintegrated
7. dissimilar
8. dissociate
9. discard

F. Other Prefixes
Exercise 1
Answers will vary.

Exercise 2
1. impolite
2. irrelevant
3. informal
4. illegible
5. irresponsible
6. incurable
7. unfamiliar
8. untrustworthy
9. unpopular
10. immature
11. unexpected
12. unimpressive
13. illiterate
14. incapable
15. insignificant
16. illogical
17. irreparable
18. illegitimate
19. irreversible
20. impure

Exercise 3
1. nonstop
2. semifinal
3. bipartisan
4. nonaggression
5. nonmember
6. nonintervention
7. nonoperative
8. nonexistence
9. bicultural
10. nonofficial
11. nondomisticated
12. nonliterate

Exercise 4
1. counterproductive
2. counteract
3. counterattack
4. prearrange
5. antibody
6. postwar
7. precolonial
8. antisemitic
9. antisocial
10. anticlimax
11. antitoxic
12. prehistoric

Test on Prefixes
1. b
2. c
3. b
4. a
5. b
6. d
7. a
8. a
9. d
10. b
11. c
12. a

Chapter 10: Theme Grouping: Places and Movement

Exercise 1
1. The leaf fish propels itself using its fins.
2. The leaf fish creeps up on its prey, until with a final thrust it engulfs its prey.
3. The bat fish lies stationary among the leaves.

Exercise 2
1. Joshua is their most dynamic player.
2. Joshua wants Susan to clip the border around the walkway.
3. The tool has a very sharp edge.
4. Joshua's mother likes the hedges trimmed a certain way and there isn't much margin for error.

5. The water in the bird bath is stagnant.
6. Joshua thinks the water should be drawn out of the bird bath.
7. Susan suggests that they heave the bird bath on its side.
8. The stones at the bottom of the bird bath will scatter everywhere.

A. Boundaries and Borders
Exercise 1
1. rim
2. brink
3. rim
4. margin
5. rim

Exercise 2
1. brim
2. margin
3. limit
4. boundary
5. frontier
6. brink
7. rims
8. edge
9. border

B. Moving and Not Moving
Exercise 1
1. T
2. F
3. F
4. T
5. F
6. T
7. T
8. T

Exercise 2
1. c
2. a
3. b
4. c
5. a
6. c
7. c
8. a
9. c
10. b

C. Pushing and Pulling
Exercise 1
1. T
2. F
3. F
4. T
5. T
6. T
7. T
8. T

Exercise 2
1. c
2. a
3. b
4. a
5. c
6. b
7. c
8. b
9. c
10. a

Test on Places and Movement
1. B
2. C
3. C
4. A
5. D
6. C
7. B
8. A
9. B
10. C
11. A
12. D

Chapter 11: Theme Grouping: Size

Exercise 1
1. Hummingbirds are special because of their diminutive size and brilliant colors.
2. Hummingbirds have miniscule barbs on each feather.
3. Prolonged suspended and backward flight require about 54 wing-beats per second.
4. At night a hummingbird goes into a diminished state of energy resembling hibernation.
5. The female hummingbird builds a miniature nest.

Exercise 2
1. Jeremy went to go see the expanded dinosaur exhibit at the Natural History Museum.
2. The full-size models dwarf everything else at the museum.

3. Margaret wants to write about the decline and extinction of the dinosaurs.
4. The information at the museum will augment Margaret's library research.

A. Size: Small
Exercise 1
1. F
2. F
3. T
4. T
5. T
6. F
7. T
8. T

Exercise 2
1. a
2. c
3. a
4. c
5. a
6. c
7. c
8. a

B. Growing and Getting Bigger
Exercise 1
1. T
2. F
3. F
4. T
5. F
6. T
7. T
8. T

Exercise 2
1. amplified
2. prospered
3. prolonged
4. flourished
5. swamped
6. expands
7. augments
8. boomed
9. boosts
10. swelled

C. Getting Smaller
Exercise 1
1. T
2. T
3. T
4. T
5. F
6. T
7. T
8. T

Exercise 2
1. b
2. a
3. a
4. c
5. a
6. c
7. c
8. a
9. c
10. b

Test on Size
1. C
2. D
3. D
4. C
5. B
6. A
7. A
8. D
9. B
10. A

Chapter 12:   Suffixes
Exercise 1
1. Fearlessness, dedication, and endurance were the qualities Sally needed to complete her training program.
2. Sally was a mission specialist.
3. Robert Crippen was mission commander.
4. The mission was successful and historic.

Exercise 2
1. writer, naturalist
2. photographic
3. distasteful
4. fermentation
5. emergence
6. fierceness

A. Noun Suffixes
Exercise 1
1. signage
2. closeness
3. insistence
4. preference
5. existence
6. assemblage
7. denial
8. trial
9. storage
10. exclusion
11. persuasion
12. improvement
13. acquisition
14. seizure
15. obedience
16. emphasis
17. difference
18. recovery
19. prosperity
20. proposal
21. shrinkage
22. breakage
23. explosion
24. encouragement
25. advertisement
26. producer

B. Adjective Suffixes
Exercise 2
1. weekly
2. humorous
3. poetic
4. grammatical
5. agreeable
6. talkative
7. childish
8. tiresome
9. courageous
10. handsome
11. harmless
12. dependable
13. informative
14. grassy
15. miraculous
16. dramatic
17. alphabetical
18. regretful
19. creative
20. boyish
21. dangerous
22. mouthy
23. painless
24. hesitant
25. adjustable
26. climatic

D. Verb Suffixes
Exercise 3
1. hospitalize
2. sympathize
3. solidify
4. captivate
5. frighten
6. lengthen
7. darken
8. lessen
9. flatten
10. brighten
11. regulate
12. thicken
13. falsify
14. identify
15. liberate
16. sweeten
17. broaden
18. immunize
19. deepen

Exercise 4
1. exclude, exclusion, exclusive, exclusively
2. repeat, repetition, repetitive, repetitively
3. differ, difference, different, differently
4. electrify, electric, electrical, electrically
5. emphasize, emphasis, emphatic, emphatically
6. economize, economic, economical, economically
7. decide, decision, decisive, decisively
8. compete, competition, competitive, competitively
9. exclude, exclusion, exclusive, exclusively
10. purify, purity, pure, purely

Exercise 5
1. beautify, beauty, beautiful, beautifully
2. originate, origin, original, originally
3. free, freedom, free, freely
4. simplify, simplicity, simple, simply
5. familiarize, familiarity, familiar, familiarly
6. generalize, general, general, generally
7. organize, organization, organizational, organizationally
8. originate, origin, original, originally
9. sanitize, sanitation, sanitary, sanitarily
10. succeed, success, successful, successfully

Exercise 6
1. machine, machinist, mechanical
2. art, artist, artistic
3. politics, politician, political
4. music, musician, musical
5. electricity, electrician, electrical
6. botany, botanist, botanical
7. theory, theorist, theoretical

8. poem, poet, poetical
9. finance, financier, financial
10. science, scientist, scientific

Test on Suffixes

1.	C	6.	B	11.	B
2.	D	7.	D	12.	D
3.	A	8.	D	13.	A
4.	B	9.	B	14.	C
5.	B	10.	C	15.	B

Chapter 13:   Phrasal Verbs

Exercise 1

1. In 1908, Charles Richter and his family headed for Los Angeles.
2. "Ended up" in sentence 2 means that Richter finally, or in the end, dedicated his life to earthquake research.
3. Richter had to sign up at the University of Southern California.
4. In 1935, Gutenburg and Richter worked out a scale for measuring earthquakes.

Exercise 2

pick up, sit down, pack up, look after, stop by, take off

Exercise 3

1. take away = remove from, carry from
   take down = disassemble
   take off = leave, depart
   take out = carry away from or out of, remove
   take to = respond to, devote oneself to
2. bring down = carry forward, cause to fall
   bring in = produce as profit or return
   bring out = make clear
   bring up = rear, educate, bring to attention

Phrasal Verb Practice

Exercise 1

1.	C	6.	A
2.	D	7.	B
3.	A	8.	C
4.	B	9.	D
5.	C	10.	A

Exercise 2

1.	broke off	6.	set up
2.	C	7.	work up
3.	sprang up	8.	C
4.	stood up for	9.	put off
5.	C	10.	put in

More Phrasal Verb Practice

Exercise 1

brought to, clear up, showed off, going on, frightened by, put off

Exercise 2

part, up, on, out, out

Exercise 3

A. spread, thought, from, up, up with, out of, were out of
B. pulled through, turned out, found out, passed, place, turned up
C. set, up with, stand out, up, brought about

Test 1: Phrasal Verbs

1.	C	4.	C	7.	B
2.	A	5.	C	8.	C
3.	B	6.	D	9.	D

Test 2: Phrasal Verbs

1.	A	6.	C	11.	C
2.	D	7.	B	12.	D
3.	C	8.	C	13.	B
4.	B	9.	D	14.	A
5.	A	10.	B	15.	A

INDEX